The Whole Family of God

Bishop Lyttelton
Library
Winchester

By the same author

THE FOOLISHNESS OF GOD
(Darton, Longman & Todd, 1970)

The Whole Family of God

JOHN AUSTIN BAKER

Canon and Sub-Dean of Westminster

MOWBRAY

LONDON & OXFORD

ISBN 0 264 66596 1 (hardback)
ISBN 0 264 66733 6 (paperback)

First published 1981 by A. R. Mowbray & Co Ltd
Saint Thomas House, Becket Street, Oxford OX1 1SJ

Photoset, printed and bound in Great Britain by
Redwood Burn Limited, Trowbridge & Esher

TO THE MEMORY OF
AUSTIN FARRER
MASTER OF WORDS
LOVER AND SERVANT OF THE
WORD OF GOD

ACKNOWLEDGEMENTS

The author and publisher wish to express their thanks to the following for permission to reproduce material of which they are the authors, publishers, or copyright holders.

Faber & Faber Ltd for the 'Little Gidding' extract from *The Four Quartets* by T.S. Eliot.

Macmillan (London & Basingstoke) Ltd for four lines from *Readings in St John's Gospel* by William Temple.

The Student Christian Movement Press Ltd for the last stanza of the poem 'Powers of Good' from Dietrich Bonhoeffer, *Letters and Papers From Prison*, enlarged edition, SCM Press 1971.

Constable Publishers for eight lines from a poem by Peter Abelard translated by Helen Waddell in *Mediaeval Latin Lyrics*.

The Society of Authors as the literary representative of the Estate of John Masefield for four lines from the poem, *The Everlasting Mercy*.

If we have unwittingly transgressed any copyright, we make sincere apologies and will acknowledge any such oversights in future editions.

Contents

Preface

One of the most splendid things to happen to me during twenty-five years in the priesthood is to have been the victim of the ultimate after-sermon story. I had been conducting the evening Congregational Service in Westminster Abbey, and was saying goodnight to people as they left. A visitor from across the Atlantic came up to me and took my hand. 'Father,' she said, 'all the time you were talking, I had the strongest feeling you were trying to tell us something.'

Most preachers will wryly acknowledge the painful accuracy of that remark. If our sermons are to be of any value they must be attempts to express truth which *we* have experienced. But that experience is elusive, always changing, always developing. Never is it clear and complete, cut and dried. Never do we really understand it. We are always trying – and failing – to tell somebody something.

That is why many of us find we cannot take an old sermon out and preach it again. The words were never very good; but now they assuredly will not do any longer. What is more, a sermon is a very particular and personal thing, an exchange with one unique group of people at one unique time. How then can anyone even think of publishing sermons?

Probably no one would, unless it were urged on them with over-kindly force – in this instance by Canon William Purcell, for whose wise help in editing and arrangement I am deeply grateful. Nevertheless occasional pieces in any branch of writing may for a brief while have their usefulness; and my prayer is no more than that some passing remarks in these may help someone here, someone there. After all, the commonest experience of all preachers is that what people remember years later is not the central thought they were struggling to convey but the throwaway aside. The Holy Spirit has a private and strongly developed sense of humour.

Preface

It ought perhaps to be mentioned, however, that one major theme does emerge quite unintentionally, running through these sermons. That is the theme of the human race, indeed the whole world, as the 'family of God' – whence the title of the book. Christianity is not a special vocation for some. It is about our true situation as human beings – brothers and sisters of the Son of God – and what the life of that unique and universal family ought to be.

Lastly, a word about the dedication of this book. It is to me a matter of deep pride that I share a Christian name with one of the greatest theologians and most lovable human beings of this century, and of constant thanksgiving that I was privileged to know him a little during the later years of his life. He was also, of course, a preacher of such exceptional quality that some volumes at least of his published sermons will live on as spiritual anthologies of permanent value. To offer this book to his memory is for me a gesture of loving homage, acknowledging what preaching can be but in one's own case never will.

St Margaret's, Westminster   JOHN AUSTIN BAKER
Passiontide 1980

The Whole Family of God

1

Preached in Westminster Abbey,
4 January 1976.

Varieties of Vision

IT IS NEVER pleasant to be told our faults. And it is particularly un-pleasant when the person who is telling us gets them right. Most of us have our own picture of ourselves, with what we like to think are our strong points, and an unconsciously censored list of weak ones. We may not be quite so off the mark as the man who said, 'My fault, if I have a fault, is excessive modesty,' but we do not usually score very high. The good qualities and abilities on our list tend to be the ones we admire rather than the ones we have got, and the bad features are those which we find it easiest to admit because they can perhaps be given a certain glamour or measure of excuse.

By the same token we leave out the virtues for which other people value us, and would indeed be slightly insulted to be told we had them. 'One thing about Smith,' they say, 'if you tell him to do something, you know it will be done, properly and on time.' Now this is a rare and admirable virtue, but Smith sees his real qualities, perhaps, as bold imagination and originality. So Walter Mitty, no doubt, would have been deeply hurt to learn that his superiors thought highly of him for the pedantic care with which he followed the correct procedures in the office. And what of our real faults? What a shock it is to most of us when we suddenly realise that our greatest failings are in fact the ones we most hotly criticize in other people!

Nevertheless, though we are wrong on many points, though we leave out this and put in that, yet we are not wrong about everything. There are always some truths, often very deep inward facts about ourselves which we know and other people do not. Thus, someone may seem to all the world the soul of good company and a person with an inexhaustible store of friends, yet inside they feel terribly alone, and no one stumbles on their secret until the note is found propped against the empty bottle of tablets. Another may be written down by everyone as cold, stiff

1

and unfeeling, yet inside they burn with compassion and sympathy, which they can express only by secret and anonymous acts of kindness. Another seems to bloom and burst with confidence yet inside is for ever fighting against panic and self-mistrust. 'The heart knows its own bitterness,' said the wise man; and he was right. There are, and always will be, things about us which no one will ever know, not even those closest to us, except ourselves and God.

Saint Paul was keenly aware of this truth, and refers to it more than once. He puts it very clearly in the passage we heard as this afternoon's second lesson: 'What man knows the nature of a man except the spirit of the man within him?', he asks. Then, from this observation of a fact of life, he goes on to draw a conclusion about God: 'So also only God's Spirit knows the nature of God.' What he means is this. God is a mystery. No one knows this better than the serious religious believer. In fact those whose lives and words have shown them to be closest to God and most deeply sensitive to him – the great saints and theologians, the men and women of prayer and love and compassion – have been the most emphatic about this. The heart of infinite and eternal Being is an abyss – not an abyss of emptiness, rather one of intensest life and reality – but an abyss none the less which we can never hope to fathom. Only God himself can know all that it means to be God. So, says Saint Paul, if we do manage to know anything, if we have one authentic glimpse, however tiny, then it must be God himself who has opened our eyes to it. God's own spirit must be in us, enabling us to think and see and feel things his way.

How does this happen? In the Church today there is a great wave of enthusiasm, of faith in the power and presence of the Holy Spirit. Springing from contact with the Pentecostal churches, it has spread through every denomination, and is commonly spoken of as the 'charismatic movement', from the word *charisma*, used in the original Greek of the New Testament to refer to the gifts bestowed by the Holy Spirit. The distinguishing mark of those who belong to this movement is, as I say, their burning certainty that God the Holy Spirit is a real force, a fact in their lives that they can feel, doing wonderful things in them, through them, around them, which they can see and hear for themselves. No longer is the Spirit a mere pious theory, trotted out at Confirmations and on Whit-Sunday. Now all is as it was in the first days of the Church, in the stories to be found in the book of the Acts of the Apostles. Here and now, in our own day, people do speak with tongues, they do prophesy, they do heal the sick and free sufferers from subjection to evil forces, whatever these may be. And anyone who has studied the evidence honestly must agree that very remarkable things have happened, which are good in their effects, and which are quite different in kind from the experiences of most churchpeople and congregations.

Take the feature of the movement which attracts most attention, speaking with tongues. This means that a worshipper, in joy or adoration or gratitude, is carried away by some force within him to pour forth his soul in sounds like words but not in fact actual words in his own language. Those who have experienced this find it a tremendous release and fulfilment. Sometimes it happens that sounds which to the speaker are completely meaningless are heard by someone else present as a message in their own language. On one well-documented occasion a Jewish Rabbi, who could not decide whether or not to become a Christian, heard the ecstatic utterance of an Irishman in the congregation as a personal command to him in Hebrew to become a missionary of the Gospel. It would be possible to put forward one perfectly proper explanation of this in natural terms as a psychological phenomenon. But such an explanation would miss out the most important point, which is that through this particular kind of uninhibited response to God's love a good and creative result was achieved, someone was freed from doubt and fear and paralysis of the will into a new and whole-hearted and blessed direction for their life. There sprang into being an enthusiastic dedication to God and other people, which no amount of thought and argument had been able to achieve, however much it had prepared the way for that decisive moment. That surely is something which one can gladly describe as the work of God's Spirit.

But side by side with these good and positive things there may also be a great deal that is trivial or even dangerous. It may be a help to many uptight western Christians to release their emotions into their religion, but that can never be more than a preparatory stage. It is what follows that matters. 'By their fruits ye shall know them', said Jesus, and the fruits we look for are deeper wisdom, readier forgiveness, greater love shown forth in practical and sustained behaviour, stable and persevering joy. But the

3

unstable personality is easily led, where normal restraints are cast aside, into self-indulgence or neurotic megalomania. Charismatic gifts are natural possibilities of God's created order, and as such can be powers for good or for evil. They are not inevitably and automatically the work of the Spirit, but need like everything else to be brought under his control, if they are to work for good.

With this last statement many in the charismatic movement would disagree. They would never deny that, in St Paul's words, 'the fruit of the Spirit is love, joy, peace, patience, kindness, generosity, fidelity, gentleness, self-control.' But they would say that these other gifts – healings, prophecies, ecstasies – are equally signs of the Spirit's presence, and that only those who have received these gifts as well have received the Holy Spirit in its fulness.

To this it must firmly be said that there is only one sure sign of the Holy Spirit's presence, and that is that we become more like our Lord Jesus Christ – in values, in vision, in courage and openness of heart, in short as total human beings. Toward this goal there are many roads: some will take us through these special experiences. If the experiences speed us on our way to Christlikeness, God be praised – they are under the hand of the Spirit. If they do not, they are not.

Wherever we have 'the mind of Christ', to however small a degree – and for most of us at first it is very small – there the Holy Spirit is at work. In everyone who kneels at the crib with a heart too full to speak, and goes silently away resolved to forgive and to be at peace where before they had been bitter and resentful, the Holy Spirit is at work. In everyone who, like Mary, ponders in their heart the wonder of God sharing our human life, and suddenly realises that all men and women are brothers and sisters of the Son of God; in everyone who, in the light of that realisation, begins to shed the fears and prejudices of years and to go out in welcome toward men and women of other races and classes and beliefs, there the Holy Spirit is at work, there the nature of God is disclosed, there the mind of Christ is found among men, and the Word once more takes flesh. The Spirit remakes God's children in many ways. Let us be open to them all.

Preached in the Russian Orthodox Church
(All Saints, Ennismore Gardens), London,
on the Eve of the Feast of Our Lord's Baptism,
18 January 1975.

Our Lord's Baptism

NAKED SAVE FOR his loincloth, the young Son of God goes down into the water. Nothing sets him apart. Nothing marks him out as of any particular class or status or culture, as more or less learned or wealthy or honoured than any other human being. He is one with all men and women in the lowliness and dignity of the nature God has given us.

Nor is there anything to tell the others waiting for baptism, or the crowds come from Jerusalem to watch John at work, that this one man in the long line is indeed in one particular set apart. What they cannot see – and how should they? – is the unique holiness.

What is holiness? It is a true vision of the fatherly will of God for all men, and a total dedication to that will. These things Jesus had in a measure that no one before or since, not even the greatest of his own followers, has ever approached. But up to this moment his life had been hidden. To those on the banks of Jordan he seemed one of themselves not simply as a man but, for all they could tell, as a failed man – just as you and I are all of us in our degree failed men and women. Those who came to be baptised by John came as a sign that they repented of their sins. It seemed obvious that Jesus must be doing the same.

St Mark, whose story of the Baptism we have just heard, makes no mention of this aspect of the matter; but St Matthew is troubled. He tells us that John the Baptist, who had known Jesus well, protested: 'I need to be baptised by you. Why do you come to me?' And Our Lord replied: 'Let it be so now, for in this way it is fitting for us to fulfil all that God requires.'

What does this mean? Our Lord was indeed perfect in holiness, but he was also truly one of us. 'God from God, Light from Light, True God from True God' – yes; but also True Man, born of one who was truly a woman. And it is because he has entered fully

5

into our condition that Jesus is not prepared to claim for himself that unblemished holiness which John is ready to ascribe to him. Jesus knows that he sees and performs the will of God to his utmost ability moment by moment: 'My food is to do the will of him who sent me.' But as man he cannot know whether in his Father's eyes he has in fact done that will perfectly. Later he was to say to the rich young ruler: 'Why do you call me good? No one is good except God.' It is not possible for a man to judge himself, even if he is aware of nothing that he needs to repent. As St Paul said years afterwards: 'I know nothing against myself, but that does not mean that I am acquitted. He who judges me is the Lord.' Only God, who knows the secrets of the hearts, can judge us rightly. So Jesus, humbly and properly refusing to claim exemption from the possibility of penitence, takes his place publicly in the ranks of imperfect humanity. He speaks to us and shows us his example not from some superior and safeguarded place but alongside us. And when he does so, he receives from heaven that divine approval which he had refused to take for granted, when the voice proclaims: 'You are my dear and only Son. With you I am well pleased.'

But why did God choose this particular rite of baptism for his Son? Because water has a special significance for Man, which makes it a powerfully appropriate symbol for the manner of our salvation. Water is for us a thing ambivalent. Our remote animal ancestors came out of it, yet it is the element in which we are never truly at home. Without it we cannot live, within it we cannot live either. It is the River of Life; it is also the cruel sea, the widow-maker. And going down into the waters in a ritual of total immersion, as John's disciples did, is a symbol not only of cleansing but of that last and total surrender which is death. By the same token the coming up out of the water is a sign of rebirth, of resurrection to victorious life. By submitting his Son to this act of baptism at the very beginning of his public ministry God the Father sets forth the pattern of Our Lord's whole work of salvation: life achieved by the offering of himself in death.

So then, God's eternal Son is truly one of us. He has come alongside us without qualification or reserve of any kind. This means that God the Father offers himself to all of us as our Father. But to be able to respond, to be able to say 'Our Father', we have to come alongside the Son, alongside Jesus, to be 'one of him'. And that means, among other things, Jesus as we have seen him in his Baptism. We come first in the humility of our mere human condition, without pretensions of culture or learning, of wealth or social status, of church or race, without even pretensions to righteousness. And secondly we come ready to find true life in Jesus's own way – through death: death to egotism, self-interest, self-indulgence, self-concern, death, if need be, prematurely and voluntarily to earthly life itself.

It is well to remember that these are also our guides toward the unity that God wills for his churches. For the first and indispensable step is to recognise and confess that fellowship which does not have to be created by our own efforts but has already been created by God's own act in sending his Son to be one of us. And the second step, equally indispensable and alas, even harder, is a readiness that our own independence and our particular church preferences should die, if need be, so that a greater life may emerge.

But our goal is not just the unity of Christians but of all men and women. We know the true spirit of human unity, which the world lacks, because we know that there is already a unity, waiting to be recognised, which the human race already has because God became Man, and so every human being has the equal and infinite dignity of a form in which God himself thought and suffered, loved and died. We are all, Christians and non-Christians alike, by no achievement of our own, brothers and sisters of the Son of God. In a famous passage Turgenev says of our Lord that he has 'a face like all men's faces.' Tonight we see the glory of God in the mere humanity of the naked Christ going down into Jordan. Tomorrow let us see the glory of God in the mere humanity of every man, woman or child we meet.

3

The Priestly Calling

LET US BEGIN by looking at two pictures of the same man. He is an ordained minister in the Church of God. For our first picture we can take our choice: he is in the pulpit, perhaps, or in the chair at a parish meeting, or giving advice in his study. In each of these moments he expects to be heeded, as he does when he proclaims God's forgiveness, or hallows bread and wine in the Liturgy. Those who listen to him have many skills he can never attain, experience in human situations of which he has no more notion than a schoolboy. But he expects them to heed him, and rightly expects, because he has this duty – to unfold to them the things of God, to keep their lives sensitive to God, loyal to God. Because this is the most urgent of responsibilities, because for this he has been trained, because he has, 'as much as lieth in him, drawn all his cares and studies this way', he has authority to expect their attention, their co-operation, even their obedience. He can and should expect these things, because, as the Apostle says, 'We are ambassadors for Christ, as if God did beseech you by us.'

Now stand aside a little, and watch this same man at another moment. He is out of his dog-collar, for he is on holiday, and is in conversation with a stranger. Inevitably he is asked: 'What is your job?' Look at him: can you believe it? He is apologetic, ashamed! 'Well, actually I'm a parson,' he says, in such a tone as clearly implies, 'Please don't let it bother you! Don't turn away from me!' What has happened to our hero of the pulpit? Where, safe among his fellow-believers, he should have been humble and the servant of all, he was proud enough. Here, where above all he should be proud, he says, 'I know not the Man' – or rather, 'Yes, I know him, but I'm not really that type.' He need not worry. No one will ever think of him as genuinely a 'minister of Christ and steward of the mysteries of God'.

Never, I beg you, let the picture I have drawn be a likeness of

8

you. Never let the idol of human respect make you afraid or ashamed of what you are to be. There is no need to protest too much. Just look your questioner in the face (always do that) and say quietly and firmly, as you would state any other matter of pleasure and pride: 'I am a priest in the Church of England.'

Ordination to the priesthood is a solemn epoch in our lives, as solemn and irrevocable as marriage. To be joined in Christian marriage, impresses a character upon us. Our life can be rightly assessed only if this commitment is taken into account. So it is with the ordained ministry. From the moment of ordination onwards our life in this world is characterized by this fact. There is nothing magical about this. It is wholly personal and moral.

The question to ask yourselves, then, is this: am I glad this is to be so? Am I proud, happy, grateful that the chance has been given me to pour my one and only earthly life into this mould? to spend it in this way and no other? For, believe me, it must be 'this and no other'. Do not try to eat your cake and have it, to experience the satisfactions both of the ministry and of the world. The prevailing climate of secularized Christianity may suggest that you can, that at bottom there is not all that much difference between the lay and the ordained life, even perhaps between the good Christian and the good non-Christian life. But try to act on that principle and you will be very unhappy, and a failure at both vocations.

Ordination is a choice; and a choice means not only embracing This but renouncing That. Again it is like marriage. To marry means not only entering on much that is wonderful, but also giving up the chance of much else that is also wonderful. The man who tries to live the married state while retaining the possibilities of the unmarried misses the distinctive happiness and fulfilment of both, and his life becomes a mess. To desire to experience everything is to re-enact the Fall, to rebel against the built-in limitations of our creaturely condition, to try to be as God. We have but one life. We can do only so much. You, thanks be to God, have chosen to stake your life on the priesthood. Do it then with pride, joy, conviction.

You will, of course, have to do it through forms, methods and circumstances very different from those of your predecessors. You will, very likely, lose some of the physical tools and supports which priests like myself were trained both to use and to lean upon. If church buildings remain, and I hope they will, there will be fewer of them, and they may well be less numinous. We may have to learn to do without organs, choirs, vestments and sacred vessels, not to take refuge in ancient hallowed forms of words. More of the worship and teaching will take place in people's homes. And there will be other changes. Sooner or later we shall be working alongside women priests. Sooner or later we shall realise that intercommunion is long overdue, and that the ministers of each denomination in a particular area must combine their efforts. We shall have to trust as partners those who see and speak of Christ very differently from ourselves.

Many of you, I am sure, look forward to such possibilities with excitement. But to all of us comes the moment when we feel we just can't take any more change and the demands it makes; and that moment may come the sooner to you because the rate of change is faster.

But one thing does not change, and that is the essence of the priestly calling. What is this? It is, in the words of St Paul, 'to be in travail with' our people 'until Christ is formed in them.' The whole purpose of the ordained ministry is that in the end there should be no difference whatever between cleric and lay as redeemed and sanctified men and women. But in achieving this purpose the ministerial order has a special function. We are set apart to be wholly devoted to those spiritual concerns – teaching, counselling, absolution, prayer, worship, the sacraments, and so on – which must be alive and in full vigour if the whole body is 'to grow into the measure of the stature of the fulness of Christ.'

So many clergy today feel guilty if their life is in any way sheltered, withdrawn from the pounding of the presses, or the racket of the conveyor-belt. They suffer a sense of inferiority – that they are not doing a 'real job', that they are half-men. So they give up, and go off to do something 'useful'. Sometimes this may be right and a leading from God; but in many it means simply that they have never understood what their vocation is. Those who have to spend their days wrestling with complex technical problems, or enduring appalling working conditions to earn enough to give their families some fun in life: if these are to be good Christians, then they need help to keep the vision bright, to see what God wants of them, to have their spirits cleansed, refreshed, strengthened. Someone must be clear what it is all about; someone must be able to show them when the going gets tough that they are on the right road. And all the more so, if, as we hope, the missionary role of the laity is to increase. To expect them to do these things for themselves is to expect too much.

No doubt the priest should have more knowledge and experience of people's problems than often he does. But if he becomes immersed in the kind of life that creates the problems he will be unable to bring the Good News to bear upon them. He must manage his own life in such a way that he is vividly aware of that Good News, possessed and inspired by it. This may not rule out a part-time trade; it did not for St Paul. It may not rule out late ordination after some years spent in another job; after all, that was precisely the way, you might say, Jesus himself took. But once committed to his ministry, Jesus did not think that he had to be a fisherman in order to reach St Peter or a tax-collector to instruct Levi. It was enough, in order to help men and women, for the eternal Son of God to become a man. Once that sufficient common ground was established, their only hope lay in his concentrating all his powers, all his will, all his love in opening and submitting himself to the Kingdom: 'for their sakes I sanctify myself.' If the Gospel likewise dominates you, his ambassadors, then and only then will all be well.

But, you may say, if this is so, how can anyone approach ordination with joy and conviction? 'Who is sufficient for these things?' Surely fear and trembling are the right notes to sound?

You are right, of course, but only in a way. What you say is true from one angle, but not from every one. As you may remember, no less a person than St Vincent de Paul declared in his old age: 'Si je n'étais pas prêtre, je ne le serais jamais' – 'If I were not already a priest, I would never be one.' That is how it looks, even to the most devoted souls, when they discover what the priesthood is all about, and plumb more and more deeply their own inadequacy. (Indeed, with great respect, I would suggest that any inadequacy you may feel at present is ninety per cent theory and only ten per cent experience, or, to be cruelly precise, ten per cent observation, for your experience of the priestly life is so far exactly nil. You are not yet in a position to be so humble!)

But did Monsieur Vincent's heart-cry cause him to cancel all those Ordination Retreats at St Lazare? Did he petition the Pope to abolish the priesthood and wind up the Holy Catholic Church?

11

Of course not. And why? Because from another angle the matter is quite different. There is a job to be done, a job of incomparable importance, the effects of which reach even beyond the frontiers of Space and Time, because it is concerned with those fundamental issues that determine the eternal destiny of personal beings. It is concerned with the Truth, absolute and ultimate, that men forget at their peril. Someone has to do this job, or try to do it, if there is to be any hope – not just for humankind as a species but, far more important, for the souls alive at this moment. It is the most glorious, the most life-giving, the most joyous of tasks, as it is by an infinite distance the most essential. Once grasp that, and would we not reverse M. Vincent's dictum, and say: 'If I were not a priest already, I would move heaven and earth to become one'? Both exclamations are wholly justifiable. Both could be made at one time by one person with absolute sincerity. It depends what you are looking at. Look at yourself and you make the first. Look at the priesthood and you make the second. On what basis, then do we ever come to a practical decision?

On the basis of the grace of God, who, 'having begun a good work in you', will surely finish it, and 'equip you with everything good that you may do his will, working in you that which is well pleasing in his sight.' Indeed, it is when we have got far enough to see something of these two truths: the glory of the calling and the inadequacy of the called, that words like 'grace' begin to mean something. The very sight of the contrast is itself an act of grace in the heart. We may say of the ministry, as the Apostle says of the Christian people in general: 'Consider your own call, brothers. Not many of you were wise according to human standards, not many powerful, not many of noble birth; but God chose what the world regards as foolish to put wise men to shame; God chose what the world regards as weak to put what is strong to shame; God chose what the world looks down on and despises, what did not even exist, to overthrow what does exist, that no human being might boast before God.'

In short, this is God's regular tactic: to bring together the impotent worker and the impossible work. Let us but accept that this is so, and we can shed those false anxieties, those postures of humility at which we work so hard, and embrace our calling with joy – a strange compound of awe, exaltation, and a laughing excitement to see what God can possibly make of such a situation.

Gone for good (let us hope) are those visions of a steady and not unsuccessful progress along predicted roads, powered by those qualities and abilities which our friends assure us the Church is so lucky to have secured. However humdrum the details of your life, in the eternal dimension you are to step off *terra firma* into the abyss of heaven, where there is no up nor down, where the simplest operations of human policy become fraught with difficulty, while difficult, even impossible things happen all the time.

Look back then over all the things in your life for which you have reason to be thankful: the friends, kinsfolk, strangers; the places, books, sounds and sights of beauty; the experiences of all kinds, the memory of which brings light and warmth to the heart when it is touched; the glimpses of God. Let them all come, however trivial. *Whatsoever things are true, whatsoever things are honourable, whatsoever things are just, whatsoever things are pure, whatsoever things are lovely, whatsoever things are of good report; if there be any virtue, and if there be any praise, think on these things* – and having thought, say to yourself: '. . . and the priesthood also.'

4 Changing the World

OVER THE NEXT fifteen years, so the experts tell us, the population of the world could increase on average by 380 souls every minute: ...6...12...18...24...30... by the time this sermon is ended (and it will not be exceptionally long, I promise you) six thousand five hundred extra human beings. And all of them like you and me: that is, compounded of affection and self-assertion, wit and folly, arrogance and insecurity, and all greatly ignorant and prejudiced as to how to cope with this dazzling and dangerous world and with all the various relationships life thrusts upon us.

What a very little way one has managed to come along the road toward understanding, goodness, and love – even with every advantage, including the supreme advantage of the light of Christ and his Gospel. Perhaps many of you feel the same. Becoming reliably decent as a human being is more than a lifetime's work. What then of the millions who have no such advantages, who will be brought up on falsehood, superstition, fear, hatred, and never hear the Gospel? Yet the nature of the world we live in will be the sum of what all of us manage to make of our own brief span of life, and what we hand on to our children. There will be no changing the world that does not change these individual factors.

But what possible hope can there be of changing the world along these lines? Sisyphus and his stone had nothing on this. To get even a rough idea of the problem one would have to say that every time the boulder rolled to the bottom of the hill, and poor Sisyphus went down to start again, he found it had grown twice its previous size. No wonder, then, that human beings, realising that the world undoubtedly needs changing, have always looked for a short cut. From Plato onwards they have dreamed of creating a system in which the individual can do as little damage as possible, and be directed into acceptable ways of spending his life. But individuals have a way of being awkward; and what do you do with those who ignore or evade or defy the system?

Philosophers have tended to gloss over this difficulty, assuming that education will somehow motivate everyone to be good, by which they mean, what they regard as good. Besides, in past ages blanket enforcement of a system was not a practical possibility. Today the case is different. What today is terrifying is the alliance of modern technology with bureaucracy. In this century we have seen a sequence of tyrannies, each seemingly more irresistible than the last, and each claiming to inaugurate a new and better order of society. And many have supported these claims. After the humiliations of Versailles and the economic nightmare of the Twenties Nazism seemed to large numbers of Germans a new dawn of hope. They were able to overlook the Mark of the Beast which in the light of history is so hideously plain. Soviet Russia has brought to millions self-respect and hope which their forebears had been denied; but at the cost of a history of terror and blood, continuing to this day, which sickens one even to read, and did so long before the genius of Solzhenitsyn memorialised it.

Communist China, reliable observers tell us, has done great things for its people, and many are happy with it. But let us not forget the executions, the humiliating 're-education' of tens of thousands of little people in the communes, the anarchic terror of the Cultural Revolution, the automatic persecution of other ways of thought, not only Christian or Western but even Confucian. These things are a necessary characteristic of all systems that set out to force individual lives to fit the official programme. The Aldous Huxleys and the George Orwells saw this intrinsic necessity; and because they understood the logic of the situation, even some of their wilder flights of fancy have come true.

The aims of these tyrannies are often laudable in theory. Some even look forward piously to their own extinction. But however formidable their apparatus it will never succeed in changing the world. It can never cope with that inexhaustible cussedness of human nature which Christians call the 'fallen' state of Man. Some years ago a Moscow paper printed a very touching prize essay by a fifteen years old schoolgirl about what she hoped the world would be like in the 1980s. Her dream was that education would have removed many of the blemishes on society: people would not cheat on their bus fares, her friend's father would not come home drunk and abuse his wife. And then this heart-cry: 'Why is it necessary to die? I find the world stupidly conceived.'

Poor, dear innocent child! Witness, surely, to the natural Christianity of the human soul. What can the machinery of any government ever do to grant your deepest wishes? All it can give you is the basic necessities of life, defence against your enemies, and perhaps, if you are very talented or of great use to the Party, a country villa and a car and special privilege shopping facilities. These are not to be despised certainly, but they are not in fact what you asked for. And if you are out of step, what then? Twenty years in a labour camp or slow, devilish destruction in an insane asylum? But no government can change the human nature which continually frustrates both your dreams and its own grandiose plans, a nature of which thousands more specimens are dumped on to its hands every day. The most it can hope to do is to destroy or deactivate those rebels whom it has failed to terrify.

For the Christian there are no two ways about it. God is not concerned simply with an 'ideal' society some time in the future, but with each individual here and now. It is unthinkable for the Christian to support any system which suppresses awkward truths or propagates lies to manipulate immortal souls. Unthinkable to ally oneself with Annas and Caiaphas and Pilate to use murder and torture to suppress the dissident. Most unthinkable of all to tolerate any condemnation of human sin by a system which depends on sin at its vilest to enforce its own will. Conversely, God's realism will tell the Christian that just as our own evil can frustrate any system, however enlightened, so, where goodwill is present, any system, however misbegotten, can be made to work for happiness and salvation. We have only to think of the New Testament attitude to slavery or Jesus's own indifference to Roman rule.

Does this mean that the Christian cares nothing about the ordering of society? Certainly not. He may wish for deep and drastic change. But because he starts from God's aims for his children, and sees reality in God's light, the changes he hopes for will rarely be those proposed by human ideologies, and are most unlikely to coincide with the programme of any one political party. Equally he may see changes that are urged as indispensable to human welfare as fundamentally irrelevant, leaving untouched the real problems of mankind.

The question the Christian will ask is not: 'How can we construct a better world?' but 'How can we remove obstacles that

16

make it harder for men and women freely to choose the good?', and 'How can we create an environment helpful to such a choice?'. Let me illustrate what I mean from some topical issues. A society which allowed wealth to heap up in the coffers of a few, and at the same time left others to languish in sickness, squalor and destitution, would be hateful to God, and all true followers of Christ would fight to change it – as they did in 19th century Britain, and still need to today, both within nations and in the total international community. Or what of a society which depends on conditions of work for many which mutilate human nature and make awareness of God infinitely difficult?

But while it may be clear that particular goals demand Christian support, it may be far less clear that one politico-economic method of achieving them is more Christian than another. The three main options open to us at present are private capitalism, aiming at maximum profit compatible with efficiency; state capitalism, as in a mixed Social Democratic economy, where overall profitability is still essential though at any particular point it may be qualified by considerations of social policy; and some variety of Marxism, where central planning can in theory make profit unnecessary provided the system as a whole is in equilibrium. What Christianity does is to confront each theory with the questions I mentioned just now. Have we a better chance of removing obstacles to goodness or of creating an environment helpful to it by governmental and international control over great private capitalist systems, or by democratic control over a government which is the greatest capitalist of all, or by bringing moral persuasion to bear on a government which by definition must have total control over every facet of life? The kind of lesson we do learn, if we apply Christ's text, 'By their fruits ye shall know them,' to the history of this century, is that all programmes are vulnerable to human sin, but that the consequences of this vulnerability are the more terrible, the more that all-embracing and non-accountable power is concentrated in one section of the community.

Similarly, the Christian will be keen that all should have an equal chance of the best possible education. How this is organised may well be a thing indifferent to him. But should one system have this fruit, that it tends to give monopolistic rights to the official ideology, that it gives no fair chance, for example, of presenting Christ's truth as the best framework for human knowledge and values, then the Christian will have to fight for a system which gives real freedom to minority positions.

The world can be changed in a material way; and this can be good. Two things that might well make most people glad they were not born in an earlier age are modern drainage and anaesthetics. The world can be changed by the acquisition and storing of knowledge; and that too can be good. And the world can be changed by the quality of our own lives. Good men and women, faithful, selfless, compassionate in their jobs and in their homes do in fact by their achievements, their influence and their remembrance make the world a better and happier place. The effort to live by love *is* worth it. But the idea that we can ever create an ideal human society of universal peace, happiness and brotherly love is an illusion, long-standing, seductive, but an illusion none the less.

Christians at times succumb to this illusion. They try to promote the faith by claiming that it can succeed in this aim where other means have failed. But the claim is fraudulent, because the logic of facts means that there can never be any means by which this particular promise can be fulfilled. To God, what matters is each precious individual man and woman, made for happiness, made for eternity, learning here to live in relationships of love with other human beings and with the heavenly Father of all. And this takes time. For each individual it takes all the time there is. The world as a whole will be as good or as bad as the current state of play in this complex process allows; and the unceasing arrival of new souls makes certain that the needle will never swing to 'Good' and stay there. The human situation here on earth is an unending struggle of Light versus Darkness, of Truth versus Falsehood, or Love versus Envy, Hatred, Malice and all Uncharitableness.

That is the reality; and it may seem a grim and depressing one. But if so, this is only because we forget something which as Christians we ought not to forget: that this world is only one part, and that the smaller part, of God's reality, and that the perfection for which we yearn, and for which our struggle here is but the necessary preparation, is promised us in that new heaven and new earth wherein dwelleth righteousness, and where the controlling and ultimate reality is God Himself.

5

Children of Light

*'Awake thou that sleepest, and arise from the dead,
and Christ shall give thee light.' Ephesians 5.14*

THERE ARE, I suppose, in the lives of all of us things which we
would hate that Mary, who lives next door, or Bob, who works at
the desk next to us, should ever get to know. Perhaps they are
things past and done with. Our present life could be an open book
for all to read, but there are earlier chapters. Maybe we could
name one – or two – people whom it would be an agonizing embarrassment to meet again, or to know that our friends had met
them. Or an opportunity comes up – to go somewhere, do something, apply for a certain job – but it would mean answering sensitive questions, and to everyone's surprise we pass the
opportunity up. There are some things in life whose proper home
is the darkness, and our greatest dread is that someone some day
will let in the daylight to that room we have kept so carefully
locked.

Most of the time we can forget its existence, but not all the time.
There are odd moments when we remember. We are giving good
advice to our children, perhaps, or to an employee, to a friend or a
pupil; and we are painfully aware that what we are saying is a
case of 'Do as I say (and as I now do) but not as I once did' – only we
so rarely have the courage to admit that. We clergy, the professional dispensers of improving advice, how often we are
caught in this trap! Indeed, there is for us a more deadly temptation – our religious duty. How could people ever take seriously
the ideals I set before them, or the grace I promise them to achieve
those ideals, if they knew what a miserable record of failure my
own life really is? So, in the supposed interests of the Gospel, I pile
coat after coat of whitewash on the sepulchre of my inmost soul,
and in the end perhaps I myself come to believe that there is
nothing hidden in that darkness after all.

19

And then again, perhaps these things are not all in the past. There are those who live their lives half in the light, half in the darkness. Sometimes they endure a perpetual fear that the light may break in: every morning they contrive to be first at the letters, their heart stops when they are summoned to the manager's office, did anyone see them coming out of that particular house? Of course, if people knew all the facts, they would see that it was all justified: how could anyone manage on what they pay me? how could I survive, when life at home is so intolerable, if I didn't have some escape? But they don't know the facts, and I don't want them to. Just let me keep it dark, just that corner of my life, and all will be well. The dark is safe, I can dream there, and the world can be as I want it for once.

But the safety of the darkness is the safety of a prison, or the illusory safety of sleep. The light alone makes us free, free from fear, free from anxiety, free from neurotic delusion. There are good things in life which we do not parade or talk about, certainly, for excellent reasons of privacy or modesty or confidentiality. There are lovely things said, words which heal and encourage the sorely wounded soul, words of intimate trust and pure affection, which have no business in the public domain. But if they were made public we would not be ashamed of them. No, the rule, the wise rule for human life is clear: so live that if any single act or word of yours were made known, you would not be ashamed. Angry perhaps, hurt perhaps, but not ashamed. In the words of our second lesson: 'Walk as children of light, for the fruit of light is found in all that is good and right and true.' That is the first thing to remember: those who can live wholly in the light are free.

But we may think this applies to us, and we may be deceived. Have you ever walked into a night club in the light of morning? The place that looked so glamorous, so luxurious six hours before – now the decor is gimcrack, the furnishings tatty and stained, the whole set-up frowsty and fraudulent. There are things in our lives which we honestly believe to be perfectly all right, but when they are exposed in the full light of day, suddenly even we can see that they are not. It is rather like having a flat which is an absolute pigsty, but we muck along quite comfortably, until one day someone we want to impress comes to call, and all at once the scales drop from our eyes, and it looks too appalling for words.

Children of Light

There is an old saying, 'Live with me to know me.' Most of us are quite convinced that in our homes we are on the whole kind, reasonable, polite and considerate people. What would a hidden tape-recorder do to that conviction? Perhaps it might even justify it: there are such people after all. But for most of us there would be notes we had never suspected: the whining note of self-pity, the harshness of impatience and bad temper, the undertone of contempt, even the drumbeat of cruelty. And in the larger affairs of the world, in commerce and politics, have we not seen abundantly in these last years proof that men may do things in the dark which seem to them absolutely right, but when the blinds are drawn and the light is let in everyone can see that they were absolutely wrong?

We need the light, the full daylight on our lives, to judge and correct us. The more openly we live, the more likely we are to discern our own faults, and to shape our conduct by standards that are worthy and true. In the words of the lesson again: 'When anything is exposed by the light it becomes visible, for anything that becomes visible is light.' The last part of that sentence is strange – surely it is not the thing which is illuminated which is light? But morally it is a profound truth. For when the ingredients of our life are placed in the full light of day, then they do indeed in their turn enlighten our souls as to the truth.

But, the Christian must say, even the full light of human day, the test of total exposure to the general conscience, is not enough. In times of crisis the moral wisdom of the human community is too easily bent, too readily qualified, to make it a reliable judge. Darkness, or at least twilight settles over all decisions. We saw this in the last war. The invention and detonation of the atomic bomb saved hundreds of thousands of lives, and shortened the war by many months. But whether it was necessary to explode it over a populous city must always be deeply questionable. And most certainly there was no need to repeat the experiment. If some sort of case could be made for Hiroshima, Nagasaki remains a monstrous and unexpiated, though largely forgotten crime. So too it was with such Western episodes as the firestorm, obliteration bombing of certain German cities, notably Dresden. It served no purpose but horror. These crimes were committed by good men in a righteous cause. No one with any moral sense at all can doubt that the extirpation of Nazism was something of which even an atheist might say, 'If there is a God, this is his will'. Nor can one justly accuse the Free World, on the large view, of descending to all the methods of its enemies to secure their defeat. But there were dark episodes. There always are. Let him that is without sin cast the first stone.

Nevertheless (and this is the relevance of this ancient history) the voice, almost the lone voice of protest against the kind of action I have mentioned came, in this country from a Christian bishop, George Bell of Chichester. It is said that his speaking out of turn cost him in later years the throne of Canterbury. Be that as it may, he dramatically illustrates my last point: that when the light of human goodness fails, the light of Christ burns unquenchable and true. Again and again, when men have been wandering in a nightmare of thick darkness, they come back to the light of Christ. Christ gives the clear, unshadowed light by which we may know the truth of human affairs, not because he expounded unheard-of ideas – most of what he taught is common to what is universally best in human moral insight – but because he never deviated from his vision, he never thought or pretended that the end could justify the means.

But there is one other thing which makes the divine daylight, radiating from Christ, different from all other lights. It is not a cold light of truth and judgment alone; it is a warm and healing light of forgiveness. None of us need be afraid to come out of our darkness into the light of Christ, for that light is not condemnation but compassion and new creation. 'Awake thou that sleepest and arise from the dead, and Christ shall give thee light.' It is perhaps the supreme vocation of the Church to be the place where no man need be afraid of his own life, but where love helps us all to come out of the dark.

6

Mission

In that day shall there be upon the bells of the horses, HOLY UNTO THE LORD.... Yea, every pot in Jerusalem and Judah shall be holy to the Lord of Hosts. Zechariah 14.20–21

WHEN THE SON of God came to live in this world of ours, the nation to which he belonged had nothing corresponding to what we call a 'church', in the sense of a community of religious believers distinct from the surrounding human society. Jesus did his work in a country of which the citizens shared a common faith, rather like some Muslim states today.

Consider another point. When Jesus died on the cross, whom did he die for? We know who it was that he himself believed he was dying for: his friends and fellow-countrymen. In the words which are the living heart of this Eucharist, and for which we have the testimony of three evangelists and St Paul this is what he said on the same night in which he was betrayed, when he took bread and broke it and gave it to those same friends: 'This is my body which is given for you'; and likewise the cup after supper, saying, 'This is my blood which is shed for you and for many.' And the Fourth Gospel makes the same point when it tells of Jesus saying, 'Greater love hath no man than this, that a man lay down his life for his friends. You are my friends. . . .'

Ask St Paul the same question: for whom did Christ die? – and over and over again you get a consistent answer: Christ died for you, for us, for me. He is 'the Son of God who loved me and gave himself for me', Or again, 'while we were still helpless Christ died at the appointed time for us godless men.' This is not the time to go into the huge question of the meaning of those words, 'Christ died for us.' What we may notice is that, first, they are central to the message of God's love which the New Testament wants so urgently to give to the world; and secondly, that this is a message

23

for the world. Jesus died for *people*, just ordinary people, where they already are. As St Paul puts it: 'God proves his love for us by the fact that *while we were yet sinners* Christ died for our sake.'

One more question. Whom did God have in mind when he sent his Son to us? Whom was he trying to help? The New Testament is quite clear in its answer: 'God so loved the *world*,' writes St John, 'that he gave his only son.' And St Paul: 'God was in Christ, reconciling the *world* to himself.' And surely this must be so. If it is indeed true, as the creed in this service declares, that Jesus was the eternal Son of God, 'who for us men, and for our salvation, came down from heaven, and was incarnate by the Holy Ghost of the Virgin Mary, and was made man,' then the ones who are affected by that unimaginable event are not just the minority, those who know about it, but the whole human race. God, we are told, thought it worth while to become a human being. One of the Holy Trinity is one of us. And that makes a difference to you, to the meaning of life for you, not because you are a Christian – in fact whether or not you are a Christian – but simply because you are a man or a woman.

St Paul had grasped this, and all his life he was trying to fight his way out of the mental net of Judaism into the freedom which he sensed that this had to offer. Outside Damascus the battle in his soul between the religion in which he had been brought up and the Man whom that religion had condemned was finally settled in favour of the Man. After the crisis he went away into the desert to try and understand what had happened. When he came back one point at any rate was firm and clear and never to escape him again. What was the crucial fact about this Man? Judaism had put the Man to death, but God had raised him from the dead; Jewish Law had condemned him but God had glorified him. So the finally important thing about Jesus could not be that he was a Jew. What mattered about Jesus was that he was a human being; and so the Good News of the Cross and Resurrection, that 'God loves like that', was for everyone. As St Paul wrote some years later to the Galatians: 'There can be neither Jew nor Greek, slave nor free man, man nor woman; you are all one in Christ Jesus.' And again, to the Colossians, 'In the new life there is no difference between Jew and Greek, circumcised and uncircumcised, barbarian, Scythian, slave or free man. Christ is all, Christ is in all.'

And this surely is what the vocation of Christian, Christ-follower, is all about. If the faith in God made man is anything at all, it is a faith for humankind, a faith about humankind. It says that there is indeed a God, and, what is more, a God who has made all his children without exception for a life of mutual joy and caring; a God who asks of them no good that he is not himself prepared to do nor pain that he is not himself prepared to endure, because to welcome all these things, the good and the ill, for love's sake is the highest kind of life there is; that when we live in that spirit we live God's own kind of life and can enter his eternity. And because it says this it says more: that wherever life is lived in that divine spirit, God's kingdom is already coming, even where men do not know God nor recognise the kingdom as his.

We have therefore a twofold task. Our first and passionate concern will be to convince men of what God is really like, what he has done to help us, what he wants us to be. But alongside this we shall do everything we can to build up God's kind of life in the human family, even where we cannot convince people about God and Jesus. We shall commend God and Jesus by name as *the* Good News for mankind. But we shall also bring the spirit of God and of Jesus, as it were, anonymously into human life wherever we come, and foster and protect it wherever, because of the divine image and likeness in man, it already exists.

This anonymous Christ-bringing may or may not open people's minds and hearts to be more receptive to God and Jesus by name. If it does, that is splendid. But even if it does not, good is still done. The purpose God had in mind all along, that the brothers and sisters of his Son should live the life for which they were made, is being achieved. We must understand this. Otherwise we shall never avoid the trap of loving our neighbour not for his own sake but just in order to get him to do something else, believe as we do, become a Christian, join the Church.

So we come back to our starting-point, the Church – that Church, about which we have such mixed feelings, but which in the end we love and wish to serve. The Church has a strangely but inevitably ambiguous nature. So long as some but not all human beings know God and Jesus by name there will always be that body of people we call 'the Church'; and that Church will, in whatever form, still have its worship, its sacraments, its traditions. But the Church – like its Master – does not exist for its own sake

25

but simply to further God's plan, begun in Jesus, among mankind. Mission, declared or hidden, is not something we do to maintain or increase the institution, nor something to which we devote a small part of our time and effort because life inside the Church is so nice that we feel guilty if we do not. Mission is the sole purpose of the Church's existence, the only justification for having one at all. The Church is a means to an end, not the object of God's activity but the instrument. If the object of God's activity were to be achieved, then the Church, like the Marxist State, would wither away.

But that happy end is not yet. In the meantime it is to be your work 'to suffer the pains of bringing' God's people 'to the birth till Christ is formed in' them.

But the ministry, like the Church, is there to put itself out of business. When the world belongs so completely to God that every word is a revelation of his love; when the command, 'Do this as oft as ye shall drink it' is at last fulfilled, because every meal is a Eucharist; when every embrace is an absolution and a blessing; then every man and woman will be robed in the glory of priesthood, the true priesthood inherent in humanity's vocation in God's world. 'In that day shall there be upon the bells of the horses, HOLY UNTO THE LORD.... Yea, every pot in Jerusalem and Judah shall be holy to the Lord of Hosts'. And you will have helped to bring it about.

7

The Labourers' Reward

'THE KINGDOM OF Heaven is like unto a man that is a householder. . . .' We are all familiar with the vivid way in which Jesus sees God's nature and God's dealings with us reflected in the incidents of ordinary life. He does not idealise this life; the characters in his stories do not always behave admirably. But somehow the truth about God comes through. The story of the Labourers in the Vineyard is a case in point.

The story reflects a kind of incident that could have happened any day in Galilee, and no doubt did happen. Galilee was fertile, specialising in orchards and vineyards, enterprises that used a lot of seasonal labour. So hiring men by the day was a normal feature of life. Socially, the workforce was of two kinds: slaves, who, of course, were permanently on the strength; and free men, who earned a living either by practising a trade as craftsmen or shopkeepers or by hiring themselves out as labourers to well-off farmers or to owners of fishing-boats such as Zebedee. The men in our story are free men, which is why the householder addresses their spokesman as 'Friend', a word he would never have used to the steward who paid out the wages, and who would have been one of his slaves.

The question of pay for these labourers was one settled partly by market forces, partly by convention. The employer wanted a man who could do a certain job, and he tried to get him for as little as the man would take. This meant in theory that wages went up and down according to the amount of work available and the number of unemployed. But in fact a strict market economy in labour was moderated by a typically Jewish way of looking at things. This was their idea of justice.

By a long tradition, running right back into the Old Testament, justice was not simply a matter of defining a person's legal rights and seeing that they got them. It had a more positive and creative aspect which sprang from the deep sense that all Israel-

27

ites were brothers, rich or poor, influential or insignificant, and that no Jew could see a fellow Jew in distress and do nothing about it – something characteristic of Judaism to this day. Justice, or righteousness, meant not impartiality but a bias in favour of the under-dog. When the First Letter of John asks, 'If a man with wordly possessions sees his brother in need and shuts his heart against him, how can the love of God be in him?' it is echoing in a very Jewish way the Old Testament Law, which says, 'If there be with thee a poor man, one of thy brethren ... in thy land which the Lord thy God giveth thee, thou shalt not harden thine heart nor shut thine hand from thy poor brother.'

Now in the Greek and Roman world, the normal day's wage for a labourer was a denarius, 'penny' in the traditional English version of our story. But whereas in pagan circles this wage would normally be cut if times were hard or there was not enough work to do to fill the day, a Jewish employer mindful of the teaching of the Law might pay the full wage in any case. In other words, there was in a rough way a convention of a minimum wage which the good employer would observe: and in the story this is reflected in the householder's words to the men who were hired later in the day, 'Whatsoever is *right*, that shall ye receive.' He was not committing himself in advance to a specific sum; but the word 'right' would not necessarily mean, as *we* might expect, the proportionate sum due for the number of hours, but the minimum wage for a whole day.

If this is so, why were the workmen who had put in a full day so upset? Partly because the case was extreme: it was the last-comers whose pay made them so angry, men who had done one hour only in the cool of the evening. Also, by paying the last-comers first, and letting everyone see what they were getting, the employer seemed deliberately provocative. Had he paid the first-comers first, what he gave the last might have been accepted, if grudgingly, as charity; by dealing with the last in full view he raised expectations. It was not that the full-timers wanted the others to have less; 'they supposed that *they* should have received *more.*'

Without entering into partisan arguments about today's very different economic circumstances, it may be worth pointing out in passing that the same problem of social justice does still defeat us. The idea of a social wage, a minimum sum which every breadwinner should receive, whatever his job, even indeed if he is unemployed, is much discussed and ethically there is a lot to be said for it. But if you adopt that policy, then you cannot also have the same wide differentials between workers as you had before. The range of wages has to be compressed. If my poorer brother or sister is to have more then I must be content to take less. You cannot, like the grumblers in the story, have both a general social wage and proportionately more for yourself. The householder had gone well over the odds as it was; if he had done as the grumblers wanted, he would have quadrupled his labour costs with consequences all too familiar to us.

So the first thing to note about the story is that it is very much a real-life incident. The employer is not behaving like an eccentric and unrealistic do-gooder; this is something that could very well have happened in Galilee at that time. And no doubt, if it had, the complainers would have got the same sharp answer: 'Look here, my friend, I'm not doing you an injustice. Did you or didn't you agree with me to take the standard wage? Well, take what is yours and be off! I happen to want to give this last man as much as you. I suppose I am entitled to do what I like with my own property? Or are you jealous just because I am generous?' That is the tone of it; and any reasonable Jew in Jesus's day would have said it was justified.

But, as always, through this incident from ordinary life Jesus is saying something about God, and about what it is like to have dealings with God. What is he saying? Certainly not that all of us receive equal blessings in this life in any material sense, which Jesus knew as well as you or I to be nonsense. The point lies quite simply, as we might guess, in the attitude of the men who had worked all day. Their spokesman is blood-brother to a number of other characters in Jesus's stories who all take much the same line. People like the elder brother in the Prodigal Son – 'You know how I have slaved for you all these years; I never once disobeyed your orders; and you never gave me so much as a kid, for a feast with my friends. But now that this son of yours turns up, after running through your money with his women, you kill the fatted calf for him!' Or the Pharisee in the Temple: 'I thank thee, O God, that I am not like the rest of men, greedy, dishonest, adulterous. . . . I fast twice a week; I pay tithes on all that I get.' And so here: 'We have borne the burden and heat of the day; what do you mean by making these others equal to us?' And in all these stories Jesus is saying the same thing, something that needs repeating over and over, especially to good and decent and religious people: if you think that by your prayers and your good life you are going to secure a special place in God's love, you are wrong. The kingdom of heaven is not run on wages and promotion and rewards. God will give the last-comer as much as he gives you. His kingdom is not a farm nor a factory but a family.

When we were children, most of us at some stage thought that we could get a special top place in our parents' affection by behaving better than our brothers and sisters; and in case they hadn't noticed we probably pointed the fact out to them. But they would not have been really good parents if they had let that make any difference, if they had really loved us more or the others less. As we grew up, let us hope, we realised this; but sometimes people don't, and they carry this attitude into all their relationships, even with God. 'You ought to love me; look what I've done for you.' We degrade everything to a matter of pay.

What is the result? An anxious fear lest we should somehow fail to perform well enough in the end, like those poor business executives in some firms who are sacked if they fail to meet their ever-increasing sales targets. And correspondingly an end to all thankfulness and freedom and delight. The elder brother, the Pharisee, and the workmen in the vineyard have this in common: there is no joy in their hearts. Joy is something that comes more easily to the Prodigal, the Publican, and the late-comer who puts in an hour and goes home with an unexpected whole day's wages in his pocket. Why should this be? After all, can one not work the whole day and still rejoice? Certainly. But only if we remember what our reward really is. For God's love is so great a thing that no one can ever earn it; and so great that the least touch of it is more than all we could possibly want. Sadly it is so often only the late-comers, who couldn't possibly earn anything worth mentioning, who see that this is so.

8

Partnership

WE HEAR A great deal about marriages which come to grief because the wife has no life of her own. Shut up in the limited routine of running her home, looking after the children, she has no chance to develop her mind and personality. Her husband becomes absorbed in his career or his interests, takes for granted the setting she provides for him, and has little time or concern for her. So one day she breaks out of her dreary prison, much to his surprise and indignation, and another dream is shattered. If only, the onlookers say, he had encouraged her to be an individual in her own right, all this bitterness, and the damage to the children, might have been avoided. It all started so well and looked so promising.

We also hear a great deal about marriages which come to grief because the partners each have too much life of their own. Both had promising careers when they married, and because they were being very mature and respecting each other as real people (and perhaps also, just a little, because neither was prepared to adjust their career or be less successful than they might have been in order to bring their lives closer together) they continued with increasing momentum on their separate paths. Before long they were seeing each other only for a few hours in each twenty-four, then not for days at a time, then not for weeks. And one day they each wondered, 'What's the point?' Yet it had all started so well and looked so exciting.

And of course there are just a few marriages (though one doesn't hear very much about them because neither husband nor wife *does* anything worth mentioning, and so attracts no attention unless they happen to be in the kind of social set that interests the Hickeys and Dempsters of Fleet Street) where the partners have no interest except in each other. They may have a lot of money or a little, but however much it is, it is enough to make them independent by their own standards; and so they pass the months in happy mutual absorption with only a mild social

31

interest in events or people outside. But whether because no human being is really profound and fascinating enough to stand up to such exclusive contemplation (especially if he or she never does anything) or because suddenly some new explosive force breaks into the spell, and in the person of an outsider, attractive because unknown, tears one or the other away, this too comes to grief. And the one abandoned wonders tearfully 'Where did it all go wrong?' It started so happily and seemed so eternal.

A life of one's own, no life of one's own; wrapped up in each other, taking each other for granted; fulfilled in the marriage partnership, fulfilled outside it. Whichever way you play it, it can still go wrong. What is the answer? Is it to take great care to strike a balance, to have some individual areas of fulfilment but also to have time and interest for each other? Well obviously. But to say that is only to repeat the advice of every 'problem page' in every magazine. It is true so far as it goes. But in an odd way it overlooks something that can be found in every successful marriage, and which happens only when we look at the situation in a completely different way. If you start with the question, 'How do you take two individuals and help them to succeed in the job of living together as a permanent partnership?' of course it is terribly difficult. Too much in one direction and someone is stifled, starved, loses their identity; too much in another and there is no real partnership, no mutual enrichment. Even the partnership itself, as we saw, can be too all-devouring. Spend too long gazing into each other's eyes, and it goes bad. No wonder some people say marriage is a trap, a destructive illusion.

Yet on all sides, even today, what do we see? Successful, happy marriages. Why? Because people with intuitive good sense have grasped the truth behind all successful partnerships, which is this. There is no point in forming partnership simply in order to form a partnership. *You form a partnership in order to do something else.* Bryant and May, Morecambe and Wise, Lindwall and Miller (for the middle-aged like myself), Gilbert and Sullivan, St Francis and St Clare, the Curies, you can go on and on and on. And thousand upon thousand of unknown examples are all around us. What keeps people in harness even when their temperaments clash violently and things go badly wrong is the fact that there is something they both want to do and which they can only do, or do best, when they do it together. In what is today, alas, a word too often derided, they are a 'team'.

Every good marriage knows this intuitively. The partners do not say, when the idea of marrying crops up, 'If we were together, I would no longer be able to do this or that'. If either of them says that, he or she had better leave marriage alone. Those who know in their bones what marriage is about say, 'If we were together, how much more we could do.' This is not – please note – the same as a man saying, 'If I were married and had someone to run my home and love me and entertain my friends, how much more successful I would be.' Nor as a woman saying, 'If I were married and away from home and didn't need to have a job, what fun I could have!' It is not a matter of what *I* could do, but of what *we* could do. This may be a professional or vocational alliance. For most people it is primarily expressed in making a home and bringing up children. But the point is that they see each other as complementary. Whatever they have in common, each also has gifts the other has not got.

So, given a shared purpose, they pass the ball back and forth. Dad or Mum (as the case may be) comes in and says, 'Those people at No. 34, the wife's had to go into hospital. What can we do?' The phrase 'What can *we* do?' is typical and significant. It recognises that the marriage partnership has created a new fact, a dual person, if you like, which can do things for others that neither could do separately, and yet that each partner is an individual with a unique contribution to make. But this gives greater flexibility too. Because the partners operate as a unity, each can fill in for a wide range of the other's normal jobs if necessary. The whole point is that neither thinks 'How can we make this a team?' You start from the fact that it is a team, and the team is involved in everything either does, and that is how the individual finds fulfilment, and the partnership stability.

But I have not been saying all this only as a kind of marriage guidance but also as a parable. For this sense of partnership, of which marriage is a prime example, is something that applies to all human life. We are all bound up in the bundle of life together. We all belong to various 'teams' – at work, in our neighbourhood, in our leisure activities, as citizens of a nation, as members of a church congregation. And we know, too, how much better things go when the fact of the team is taken as the starting-point for our attitudes, when we ask, 'What can *we* do?' To take but one obvious example, how much faster and more deeply does Christian unity develop when Christians of various denominations ask 'What can we do, as a team, for our fellow-men, here in this city, or in a deprived area of the world?' What is called the problem of the church in the 'inner city' can certainly be resolved in no other way. Denominations wondering how to unite get nowhere. Christians wondering how they can help the life of an area like Westminster or Brixton or Camberwell find they are already deeply united. What matters as in marriage is to stand side by side and look outwards as much as to stand face to face and look at each other. And finally this is the secret of partnership with Christ. Writing to the Corinthians, St Paul paints this graphic picture of the Christian as part of a body; like a foot or hand or eye each of us has something to contribute which no one else can give. All are necessary, all are distinct. But the body as a whole, that is Christ.

If you want to make that union, that partnership with Christ a reality, you will not spend all your time looking inwards at Christ and yourself. You will also stand beside him, and look out at the world with his eyes, and ask 'What can *we* do today?' Part of the answer will always be to do the routine jobs as well as possible; but another part will be some new thing, probably quite small, which we never noticed before, but which we notice now because we are thinking as a member of Christ's team in this situation. And if we do everything with the love and care that comes naturally to those who work alongside him, then in that partnership we shall find more and more fulfilment as individuals, and also a stable friendship which will endure into eternal life.

9 Temptation

ST FRANCIS OF Assisi, so the story goes, once spent a whole Lent, from Ash Wednesday to Maundy Thursday, on an uninhabited island in the lake of Perugia. And so earnest was his desire to be like Christ in all things that he took with him for food only two small loaves, and of these in fact ate but one half loaf.

The forty days that Jesus spent in the wilderness have inspired many Christians down the centuries to take the same trail. They are supposed, each Lent, to inspire us – in our own small way. What do we expect to get from following him here? The promises are familiar enough: a deeper spiritual life; a new understanding of the faith; new ways to serve God and our neighbour. A refresher course in discipleship, in fact. The one thing we are not promised is the one thing that according to the Gospels Jesus did get out of it: temptation.

But is not that very fact rather strange? How could Jesus have been tempted, if he really was the perfect man Christianity makes out? Surely a really good person wouldn't feel the tug of evil?

There is truth in this objection, even though it is only part of the truth. Some sorts of temptation do leave us alone much of the time, as we grow into better human beings. Such temptations as vanity, lying, or the grosser sorts of inconsiderateness. You can become, for example, someone who genuinely wants to spare others pain. So it is true: a really good person will not be greatly bothered by some of the things that throw you and me.

This doesn't mean that such a person won't have the same feelings: but their feelings don't prompt them to what is wrong. Jesus felt thirst, and asked the woman of Samaria for water. But when, instead of giving it to him she started a long theological argument, he didn't become angry or resentful. He responded to her need. Again, Jesus must have felt sexual desire. But he didn't let it divert him from what he was supposed to be doing, or use it as a comforter to keep the cruel world at bay, or plan to satisfy it re-

35

gardless of the good of others. Desire is not the same thing as temptation.

Temptation comes when we are so divided in our vision of life, so uncertain of our calling as human beings in this or that situation, that we let our desires have a status they are not meant to have. Most of us have a long way to go before we grow beyond this condition, where temptation *is* a sign of something wrong, and where not just our physical desires but our emotional needs – to be well thought of, perhaps, to be important, to be in charge, or just to be left alone – still run the show.

Jesus, when we meet him in the Gospels, seems to be past that stage. But even so that does not free him from temptation.

He went straight into the wilderness from his Baptism, where he had heard the voice from heaven confirming his sense of special vocation. God had some unique work for him. What was it? He had been moved to go to John. One step usually led to another. Where was the next clue?

Out there, in the desert. Some people can't stand being alone even here, amid civilisation. The desert is a yet sterner test. As a recent article on the desert put it: 'Only experience teaches how to cope with the natural loneliness and fear . . . Anxieties have to be overcome with an effort of will . . . The desert is a confrontation with absolutes . . . and with the fact that this universe does not mock us. It is no coincidence that monotheism comes out of the desert.'

So Jesus has to be balanced and strong to cope. He is open to the voice of the silence. And that voice gives him a vision, a vision of what the world might be. A world where we live not by bread alone but by *every* word that comes out of God's mouth: that is, where God is trusted, and the world he has given is accepted, with all its mysteries and dark problems, as ultimately for our good. A world where the only way forward is purity of heart, the determination not to use evil that good may come, where the end never does justify the means, whatever the appearances.

This vision is clean, clear, simple, cutting like a sword of light through all the clouds of doubt and perplexity. Jesus is captured by it. Now he knows his vocation – to give this vision to the world before it is too late. This is what the voice meant when it said: 'Thou art my beloved Son.' God's Son is one who lives by total trust in God as Father and so in the sufficiency of God's world for our destiny. He is the Son in order to make others sons and daughters, to teach them to say, 'Abba', 'Father'.

Now it is a well-established fact about solitude that it suddenly becomes peopled with dark forces that spring up – where from? – to challenge us. Once we are seized of a vision like that of Jesus, it seeks to impose on us its particular order, to harness our whole self to its creative purpose. But the self, the vitality within us, has its own goals: survival and satisfaction. The purposes that come through the mind and soul, from God, cut across these, and try to turn life out of its natural channels. At once the energies within us burst out in an attempt to escape the constraint of the vision, to return to their own spontaneous way. The vision Jesus had received was making huge demands upon him. In the process of growing into obedience to these divine demands there was a struggle in which the natural forces within him tried to reject the new pattern, and in the silence of the desert, in the emptiness, were projected outside him to challenge him from there.

The challenge turns on his sense of personal vocation: 'If you *are* the Son of God' – playing at once on natural pride and natural doubt. If you are this special person, then you can make your own rules. The job is what matters, getting the vision across. Use any means to hand: look after yourself ('It really won't do working so hard, going without rest, you must take care of your health!') – get worldly power ('Of course you'd be a fool to turn that job down, think how much more influence you'll have!') – play on people's lower motives ('What matters is to get people behind you!'). God has left it all to you: so you make up your own mind.

This temptation arises from wholly good things – a true vision, a true vocation. Jesus's reply is that he must himself be subject to the vision or the whole thing is a fraud. *He* must trust God's world, *he* must trust God's methods.

There is a fearsome challenge here to us Christians, who are always preaching to others more than we have proved in our own selves. Our first priority is to expose ourselves to that vision, to go into the solitude where God is and precious little else, to learn to cope with the proper loneliness and fear this produces, to face the explosion of our natural selves which come rushing out, saying, 'Anything but that!' We train ourselves in worship, in Bible study, in counselling, in social ethics, in prayer, in anything but the underlying rock-thing on which all else must be built: this vision of God, of the sufficiency of his world, of trust, of refusal to do evil that good may come.

The object of so much of our striving is to give everyone techniques, and to call that 'the ministry of the laity.' The same techniques that have not notably succeeded when used by the clergy. This Lent forget them. Instead look at the world as it is and say, 'O God, is this all? Is this what I have to trust? Am I to cope with this by using only love, truth, forgiveness?' Put that way round it may make the vision burst upon you with terrible clarity, and provoke that eruption from within which must come before we grow up to be integrated children of God.

We can, of course, stand only a little of the desert at a time. Yet once we have seen something of the vision, caught some of God's words, we always want to go back, to find more, because anything else seems so second-rate, such a waste of our short and precious time.

One thing more. This experience, once you have had it, tells you Christ was right. It also tells you how far beyond us he is. Take his vision seriously, and you find yourself worshipping him ... not as God but for his human achievement. That is important. If he were naked God, there would be infinite room for us to pride ourselves on our limited human successes. But God doing it our way, and shunning pride into the bargain, that leaves little scope for self-satisfaction. The monkish chronicler says that St Francis ate the half-loaf to cast forth from himself the poison of vainglory. He was right, but not, I think, in the sense he intended. St Francis ate the bread, I believe, not lest he should think himself as holy as Christ, but because his forty days showed him how far he still fell short of Christ. But we shall go farther by that falling short than on any journey of our own.

10

The Breaking of the Bread

'Do this in remembrance of me.'

IF ANY OF you have stayed with Jewish friends at a weekend, you may have had the privilege of being present when the Sabbath prayers are intoned and the Sabbath candle lit. And it may have struck you how natural it is to the orthodox Jew to express his faith in that way, there in the everyday context of his own home.

The Jews, as we know, have been victimised and persecuted more savagely than any other people in history. In Old Testament times their country was twice devastated and its people deported. Under the pagan Roman Empire their Temple was destroyed, and they were banned from their holy city. When the Empire became Christian, they were persecuted by the Christians. In mediaeval Europe they were hounded as Christ-killers; in modern Europe they were everywhere the targets of anti-semitism, until the holocaust under the Nazis finally made Europeans ashamed. They were persecuted in Tsarist Russia; and since the Revolution they have been persecuted by the Communists. But they have this incredible gift of bringing good out of evil – they had to have, I suppose. And one of the good things they developed was the gift of domestic religion. Partly because the Jewish Law which governs every department of life was a religious obligation; but partly also because many of their sacred rites and acts of worship had to take place in the privacy of the home. There was nowhere else.

The greatest of all the occasions which the Jewish people have kept in this way in their own homes is the Passover. Here is celebrated the deliverance of their ancestors from slavery in Egypt, the real birth of the nation. The father presides at the meal, asks the youngest child the prescribed questions about the story of the great escape – for every generation must have that story by heart

– and says the prayers and the blessings. And it was on that day or the day before, in the year 30 AD, that Jesus presided over his last meal with his friends, and asked them to do one particular thing in remembrance of him.

We have to say, 'on the day of the Passover or the day before,' because we do not know, and almost certainly never shall, whether the Last Supper was the Passover meal or not. Matthew, Mark and Luke say it was; John says it was not. What is certain is that Jesus died at Passover time, which is why in Christian tradition from the New Testament onwards the story of the first Passover, the escape from Egypt, has very naturally been used as a symbol of that liberation from the tyranny of evil and death which so many have found in Jesus.

Anyway, whether it was the Passover meal or just their last chance to be together, let us go back for a moment to that Upper Room and to Jesus's words: 'Do this in remembrance of me.' Do what? say a blessing over the bread, break it, and give a piece to each person present; say a blessing over the wine, and pass it round for each to drink. This may well have been a regular custom of Jesus when he and his friends were eating together, and something he did in a characteristic way, for the two disciples from Emmaus who rushed back to Jerusalem the first Easter Sunday evening to say that Jesus was alive and had been with them reported that 'they had recognised him in the breaking of the bread.' Certainly his followers did not suppose that he meant them to do this only at Passover time, for in the Acts of the Apostles we are told that the first converts 'devoted themselves to the apostles' teaching, to the common life, to the breaking of bread, and the prayers.'

This breaking of bread took place, we are told, 'at home', in the setting of the family and household, just as Jesus's own meals with his disciples, and the Last Supper itself, had been private and domestic. But when the Christian movement spread out into the pagan world, all this gradually changed, and the breaking of bread in church became the Christian counterpart of the worship offered to the gods in the temples and shrines of other religions, something very different from what it had been originally.

Now this, I think, was a tragedy. It may have been inevitable – for a congregation of slaves, for example, who had no homes of their own – but it brought into Christianity that fatal distinction between the sacred and the secular, the church and the world, the religious and the everyday, which has done more than anything else to frustrate what Jesus was trying to achieve.

There is nothing in any of the Gospels to suggest that Jesus meant to found a new religion. He already had a religion. He was a Jew; and a Jew he lived, and a Jew he died. But the interesting thing about the Jews is that they were, so far as we know, the only instance in the world at that time of the body politic and the worshipping congregation being one and the same. The setting within which Jesus operated was that of a civil community whose members all worshipped the one God of heaven and earth. His mission to them was to deepen and purify their idea of that God, to teach them to pray to him and trust in him as Father, to seek his forgiveness, and to obey him first and foremost in unselfish love of all other men and women. It was for this purpose that Jesus called his followers to be the salt and the leaven and the light in the world. His vision was of ordinary life as sacred, which was why he cared little for the tabus about ritual purity, sabbath observance, and so on. And it was wholly in line with this attitude that he should seize on the Jewish insight about worship in the home, and that the only observance which he enjoined on his friends to keep their devotion to the cause alive was one which was a natural part of everyday living. 'Do this in remembrance of me.'

It is ironic that Christianity of all movements should have lost hold of this principle. For the central belief of the Christian creed is that in Jesus God himself shared a genuine human life and death. You may or may not accept that belief. Personally I am firmly convinced that it is true, and if we had a couple of hours or so it might be possible at least to explain the reasons for this conviction. But whether you believe it or not, you can, I am sure, see the kind of implications that would follow from such a belief. For one thing it would mean that all men and women everywhere, whatever their religion or philosophy, their race or culture, whether or not indeed they had even heard of Jesus, were brothers and sisters of the Son of God. In other words, that the one family of God is the human race as a whole, not just the Church. It would also mean that ordinary human nature and ordinary human life have the potential at least of expressing the character of God, that in our human state even God could be himself. This

41

is, or ought to be, the vision to which Christians are committed; and their calling is to help all men to realise that this is so.

There are many ways of going about this. One of the most important is to cultivate the gift of 'thinking human', of realising that for all the failures and evil of which men are capable, they also have this family likeness to the Son of God, and that in our work, our responsibilities as citizens, our home life, our neighbourhood, we shall have endless opportunities to work together with others just as human beings to foster and protect this spirit of Jesus. And another area for action is the one we have been thinking about – that awareness of God, that sense of the divine dimension to human life, which we call 'worship'.

Christians everywhere today are undoubtedly striving to reintegrate worship and life. The new flexibility and freedom which marks services in every church; the 'house church' with its Eucharist on the kitchen table, or the Eucharist in the factory canteen – these things are all signs both of an unease and of a desire to do something about it.

But such measures by themselves will never be enough. They are still trapped in the mental categories of the immemorial separation between the sacred act and the profane human reality. All that they do is to move that sacred act physically into the setting of the profane reality. They do not unite the two. To achieve that unity something much more radical is required.

One vital Christian contribution to human life is Christ's own gift of bringing all life within the sphere of the sacred. The joy and thanksgiving that come with penitence and pardon, prayer and sacrament must not be confined to the cultic enclosure and the priestly caste but must come into the lives of all men wherever the life of God's world finds them. When a Christian family can welcome into their home someone, of whatever faith or philosophy, with whom they have been working and thinking and suffering for the benefit of the whole human family in their town or village or country, and share with them as honoured guests the bread that has been broken and the cup which has been blessed as the heart of the family meal, then Jesus Christ the eternal Son and Brother will be present in the midst not just of his Church but of his world.

11 Renewal in the Parish

WHAT IS A parish? It may be anything from two score homes in a village to several thousand in a wilderness of housing estates; a series of gaunt high-rise flats, or bulldozed wasteland never rebuilt; office blocks, shops, warehouses or factories, teeming by day but at night occupied only by watchmen and cleaners. But, whatever the scene within that arbitrary line on the map one thing remains the same. The line is there because it identifies *people*. Parish = People. They may be elusive; their attachment to that particular area may be very thin; they may hate it rather than love it; they may be fluid, migrant, constantly changing. But they are what the Parish is about. The whole purpose of the Parish system is to include people, all the people, to make sure that in the whole network of parishes all over the country everyone belongs somewhere.

But in another sense a parish is not that at all. It is just a very few people who meet week by week in a building, usually rather old in its architecture, sometimes beautiful, sometimes ugly, sometimes totally unmemorable, large, small, warm, cold, full of memorials of the dead and strange furnishings, stocked with books no one else reads, where they go through rituals no one else understands led by one or two men and women in clothes no one else would be seen dead in if you paid them.

But these people are haunted by a thought, a picture, a demand that will not leave them, little as they may understand it or, at times, want it. This thought, this vision keeps shifting, it is hard to keep it clear or in focus; the demand too is hard to pin down, to know what it means in practice. But always, on the edge of it or behind it or on rare and joyful occasions, there in the middle of it are God and a man called Jesus. And they know that these two, God and Jesus, are in some way the things in life that are centrally and eternally important, not only to them but to everyone, if only they could make this clear.

And so the people who make up the parish in the narrow sense

43

can never quite forget the larger community. After all they belong to that too. They are in this particular building, thrown together with these particular fellow-Christians, only because they live or work within that line on the map. And therefore, from time to time they try to get these neighbours of theirs to share this sense that God and Jesus matter. And the neighbours themselves, niggled by an inaccurate folk-memory that once everyone did share this sense, feel just ever so slightly guilty about that strange building, and the fact that they don't really care what goes on in it; and perhaps a few of them give it a try for a bit. And then you have what is called 'renewal in the parish'. To put it this way may sound like merely cruel sarcasm. But even that minimal, despairing picture has within it all we need for genuine renewal beyond any of our dreams. It has the basic fact of *people* – people who belong together at a natural, human level because they inhabit the same small patch of this planet. Their children go to the same schools, their sick are cared for in the same hospitals, they buy their food in the same shops, suffer the same tyrannies from those wrapped in the insolence or indifference of office, catch the same viruses, grumble at the same weather, bid farewell to their dead at the same crematoria. And the key to renewal is what we as Christians believe about this aggregation of people of whom we are part.

At the heart of all our puzzles and fears and anxieties there is, if we are Christians, one small flame of joy which can never be put out: it burns on our knowledge that we human beings do not have to search for God – God has come to us. God, the ultimate meaning, the true goodness, the inexhaustible and satisfying beauty, has shared our life. He came unbidden, unpaid. By his own unilateral act he entered into the tissue of human birth and kinship and death. He became one of us, and we are his relations, brothers and sisters of his Son, whether we know it or not. The whole human race is the family of God. Not just those who have been baptised or who live a special kind of life or who hold certain beliefs. Everyone. When you go out of this church this morning the first person you see washing the car or gardening or going along to the pub is a brother or sister of Jesus and through Jesus a child of God. It is not the Church which is the family of God. The Church is that part of God's family which knows that it is part of his family, knows that all human beings belong to that family.

Now what does the Church do with that knowledge? On the answer to that question everything depends. Get it wrong, and renewal will never happen.

The wrong answer is: We must go out, on fire with this knowledge, and convince people that it is true. Then they will turn to God, and the Church will become a living power for good once more. I said, This is the *wrong* answer. When St Matthew gave it as the climax of his Gospel, it was the right answer: 'Go forth ... and make all nations my disciples; baptise men everywhere in the name of the Father and the Son and the Holy Spirit.' It was the right answer then, because that was a world which believed in God or the gods, where everyone, more or less, shared a vision of things in which the supernatural was real and important. In such a world the Gospel was able to be revolutionary, to call forth enthusiastic loyalty or violent dissent, precisely because the words meant something. Today, in a world where people believe largely only in what they can experience for themselves, there is no shared vision of reality, the words mean little or nothing. People probably think they know as a matter of theory what the word 'God' refers to; but it is not something they take any account of in day-to-day living. There is nothing solid about it.

In such a world to preach the Gospel – or to start by preaching the Gospel – is a waste of time. It is to start at the wrong end. The Kingdom of God can no longer break in through words. It must break in through experience. That means that what we do with our knowledge is not to try and share it, not at first, but to put it to work. The right answer to the question: 'What do we do with the knowledge which, as Christians, we have of the truth?' is this: to make God's Kingdom, his sovereignty, effective in hiddenness, to make the values of Jesus prevail in society anonymously. Then, when these things have in this way become for men a matter of experience, there is a chance for God to become real; and then we can talk about him in a new way which will make sense, and to that people will respond.

And what was it which we said was the foundation of God's Kingdom, the thing he did in Jesus? He made the whole human race, good and bad alike, his own family, by becoming one of us. So what then is our task? To make *that* true in experience. And because the word 'God' has so little real meaning, we have to start with the word 'family'. We have to work and pray, to suffer and love, to make the chance aggregation of humans in our parish into a family, a true community united by real human involvements and relationships. That is the top priority for any congregation: the creation of community in the whole human family in the place where we are.

Once we accept this, once we really believe that this is what our God-given time and talents and resources are for, then strange things happen. We discover that though we claim to love our neighbours, perhaps we know next to nothing about them. We discover also that we are not the people with all the ideas needed to put the world to rights, and that bringing in the Kingdom often means working humbly, just helping non-Christians who know a great deal better than we do. We may find ourselves dragged – horror of horrors! – beyond simply doing good into political questions and activity, where our contribution is made all the more difficult and stressful because we agree with no ready-made party lines.

But we also discover other things. We find a new reality in prayer, both corporate and private, because there is now such a flood of needs and problems to bring to God, such unexpected goodnesses to thank him for. We find ourselves forced back to think far more deeply what the will of God is for today, what are the values of Jesus; and we begin to search the Scriptures not as a kind of adult education exercise, something good for us, but because we desperately need to know. In our perplexities we turn also to what other Christians have discovered and told in books, magazines or whatever.

Above all, we find ourselves forced to turn to each other, not just the fellow members of our own church, but other Christians as well, to become ourselves a real community; to seek in each other help with things we cannot handle, comfort in failure, advice or at least discussion where we don't know what to do, rejoicing when God has won a point and his family has become somewhere a tiny bit more real. No longer do we sit around asking, What shall we do this autumn, or this Lent? Programmes make themselves: the first question we have to tackle is not, 'What should the Church be like?' but 'What should a real community be like?' And our worship, that is best of all; because we find we cannot bear not to come together here in Eucharist. Jesus has become real to us in his brothers and sisters, and so our hearts are opened to his Real Presence in this Communion. And when all this is happening, we may not yet have found numbers or success or income, but we shall certainly have found renewal both as a parish and in our own souls.

12 Jesus the King

*'Blessed is the King who comes in the name of the
Lord!' St Luke 19.38*

THERE HAS OF recent years been a determined attempt by some
writers to prove that Jesus was a nationalist revolutionary
leader, somewhat of the type so familiar to us from Africa, Asia
and South America. They point to the fact that one of his disciples
was called Simon Zelotes, 'Simon the Zealot', and that there was
a revolutionary movement called 'the Zealots' in Palestine at the
time, aiming to drive out the Roman conquerors. The nickname
of another disciple, Judas Iscariot, may be a Jewish form of
sicarius, the Latin word for a member of a league of assassins who
murdered foreigners and those Jews who sympathised with
foreigners. They draw attention to the story of the Feeding of the
Multitudes, when according to Mark 5,000 men sat down in military formation, in 100 groups of 50, and, according to John, the
crowd afterwards tried to seize Jesus and proclaim him King.
And, of course, there is the story of Palm Sunday when, as we
heard in the lessons this morning, Jesus fulfilled the old proph-
ecy of Zechariah, 'Lo, your King comes to you; triumphant and
victorious is he, humble and riding on an ass, on a colt the foal of
an ass.'

The last 200 years have seen many attempts to produce a new
picture of Jesus, proving that he was in fact an early case of whatever is the fashionable cult-figure of the moment. But they have
all turned out to be fairly thin, and this is no exception. The word
'Zealot' does not prove that the apostle Simon was a member of
the revolutionary movement, since the same word is used in the
New Testament of other people, like St Paul, who were nothing of
the kind; and in any case there was very little revolutionary activity in the years the Gospels tell of. If the name Iscariot does
mean 'assassin' (and that is far from certain) he is a very bad

example to prove a case about Jesus, since he was the one who lost his faith in Jesus and betrayed him to the authorities. The crowd at the Feeding of the Five Thousand may have tried to proclaim Jesus as King, but what we also know is that Jesus escaped from them, and made sure that this sudden burst of mad enthusiasm came to nothing. And, of course, when Jesus did ride into Jerusalem, he rode on an ass, which was a sign that he came in peace. Had he come in war he ought by tradition to have used a horse.

But the absolutely decisive proof that Jesus rejected any idea of leading a violent revolutionary movement – quite apart from all his teaching about loving one's enemies and not resisting evil – is that after Easter, when his followers were filled with enthusiasm and faith in his conquest of death, they made no effort whatever to start such a movement on their own. There never were more peaceable, law-abiding and submissive citizens of the Roman Empire than the first Christians. They were martyrs not militarists; and the lesson they learned from Jesus was brotherly love toward all men and an end to the old Jewish nationalistic dreams.

Nevertheless, the story of Palm Sunday does contain one note that we may find baffling, and hard to fit into our conventional picture of Jesus. In arranging for the ass to be available for his entry into the Holy City, and in allowing the crowd to acclaim him as they did, he was certainly accepting the title of 'King' in *some* sense. Perhaps the Pharisees who, as we heard, urged him to rebuke these enthusiastic followers were in fact friendly disposed toward him, felt the incident to be out of character with what they knew of him, and in any case saw how dangerous it was. They were right, too, for, you will remember, when he was crucified, a derisive notice was pinned to the Cross: 'Jesus of Nazareth, King of the Jews.' The charge that he had set himself up as a king had been made to stick, and was probably the reason why Pilate condemned him to death. So when Jesus replied to the Pharisees' well-meant advice, 'I tell you, if these were silent, the very stones would cry out', he was at least saying that it was more true to hail him as king than not to do so; and, being the shrewd man he was, he must have known very well the risk he was running when he said this. Why then was it so important to him to lay claim to the title of 'King'?

To put it in modern terms, Jesus was saying something first

about the relationship of his mission to human life in general, and secondly about the right kind of power in human affairs.

The title of 'King' is not one that relates to a purely religious organisation like, let us say, a church. In Jesus's own day there were such religious organisations. The Essenes, for example, who left us the Dead Sea Scrolls, were one such. They had, as we say, 'dropped out' of society at large, and were living in the desert in a large self-contained kind of *kibbutz*, and had nothing to do with Jerusalem or the Temple or any of the ordinary institutions of the nation. Their leaders were called 'Teachers' or 'Priests', just as we Christians have Bishops and Popes and Patriarchs and Moderators. But as soon as you accept the title of 'King', you claim a position of authority in the whole sphere of ordinary human life, authority over the nation and what we would call its 'secular' affairs. Jesus did not see his mission and his teaching as concerned only with some inner spiritual life, which might go on just the same whatever happened in the world around. He was proclaiming the Kingship of God, working through himself as its agent, over every aspect of human life.

Nevertheless – and this is the second thing he was saying – the power which that Kingdom uses to achieve its ends is not the power of physical coercion, the power of force. He came in peace, riding on an ass. Jesus was anything but a passive, submissive man, letting the world go by. He was a man of power, with great impact on the situation around him. But that power was of a very special kind. It was the power of a strong and penetrating mind, which could cut apart a bad argument in a few decisive strokes, which saw through the confusing tangle of human situations to the fundamental principles involved. It was the power of creative genius, which could put forward ideas for the transformation of human life so rich in possibilities for good that we have nowhere near exhausted them, and probably never will. It was the power of a great poet, for many of his sayings were originally in verse. It was the power of an artist in words, whose stories and parables lodge instantly and permanently in the mind and heart. It was the personal power of someone whose attitude to his fellow human beings combined the most demanding moral judgement with a compassion and tenderness toward the penitent sinner which convinced them of God's eagerness to forgive and the reality of God's love; and it was, moreover, the power of someone who established his right to take this attitude by the transparent goodness of his own character and conduct. It was also the more than normal power of one who could heal those sick in body or mind simply by a word. And it was the power of a man who had the inner resources and the faith in God to go it alone, but who nevertheless could attach both men and women to himself with a deep devotion, and who could shape and weld them into a united company to help and carry on God's work.

Power like that is real power and has no need of official appointment or coronation. Its authority shines out from within, and will not be denied. But when it is brought to bear on the whole life of a nation, when it claims authority over all our attitudes and activities, criticising and challenging prejudice and self-interest and comfortable conceit, then of course it provokes opposition and anger and hatred and counter-attack. The Gospels in their story of Holy Week show us some of the religious and intellectual leaders of the nation trying to hit back and discredit Jesus by personal confrontation, and failing utterly. In that kind of power they were no sort of match for him. So they had to resort to the other kind, the kind he could not, or rather would not use, the power of physical force. He must be eliminated.

And that seemed for a moment to work. Jesus had relied throughout on God's kind of power, the power of the spirit, and on the Cross that was reduced to total powerlessness: 'My God, my God, why hast thou forsaken me?' But, of course, that was not the end of the story. The fact that you and I are here this morning, renewing our dedication to Jesus and his kind of power, and that millions upon millions all over the world are doing the same, makes the point. The humble figure on the donkey, so ridiculously hailed as King by a ragtag and bobtail crowd, turns out to be indeed the King of a universal and indestructible Kingdom. And we are its citizens. Our calling is to use his kind of power; and to work for a world where that kind of power, the power of truth and goodness, of forgiveness and love is the only kind that is used.

13 Courage

SO ONCE AGAIN we come to Passiontide, when we think about the Cross of Jesus, and his sufferings of body and spirit, and lift up our hearts in wonder, love and praise. And what millions of words have been written and spoken down the centuries about that one event, and not just by Christians either, but by agnostics and atheists too, who have found in the story of this death *something* – perhaps they are not sure quite what – which sounded a deep echo in their souls. Nor is it just a matter of words. What about the music? What about the treasury of magnificent paintings and sculpture inspired by this instance of one of man's more horrible ways of putting his fellow-man to death? Yes, and even buildings – for the plan of a great church like this one is based on the pattern of a man – that Man – hanging on the Cross.

Many deep and wonderful things have been revealed to human hearts by gazing on this moment of defeat and nothingness – giddying insights into God himself, his unfaltering love and forgiveness to us warped and guilty creatures. Tonight I want to talk about the one absolutely fundamental human reality, without which the Cross would never have happened. And the odd thing is that this is one aspect of the whole matter which is hardly ever mentioned: I refer to the one indisputable fact of Jesus's courage.

We need from time to time to make ourselves face, however feebly, in our imagination some of the sheer physical horror of crucifixion: the nailing between the bones of the wrists and feet, the thirst, the back torn by flogging, scraping with every breath against the rough wood, and other things which it would be cruel to force on your attention now. Jesus faced these things, and recoiled from them in horror in his prayer in Gethsemane. We need to face them too, and all the more because neither the New Testament nor most great works of art are concerned to convey this side of the business. The point of facing these facts is not to make out that Jesus's sufferings were worse than those of thousands of other victims down the ages. Human beings are unique among the animals in applying their outstanding brain to the infliction of pain on their enemies. Breaking on the wheel, burning at the stake, hanging, drawing and quartering, flaying alive, the rack – just to mention a few of the routine punishments and methods of interrogation of the past, and to leave out the technological tortures, using noise or electric shock, for example, in our own century – must have been just as bad. No, at this level Jesus is one of a great and dreadful army of martyrs.

But that in itself is quite enough to make us stop and think. The prospect of physical pain is for anyone something of a moment of truth; and in our society this is a moment that comes more and more rarely. Serious corporal punishment for children is now extremely rare, and for the most part befalls only those poor scraps whose parents are liable to fits of uncontrollable temper or brutality. Birching and flogging can no longer be ordered by the English courts. There is indeed for all of us an increasing risk that we shall at some time be mugged or hammered by some group of young thugs; but with proper precautions most of us may still hope to escape that ordeal. In the realm of illness the science of relieving pain has made unbelievable strides. Even the dreaded spectre of terminal cancer has now been stripped of most of its terrors. No one now need go through the appalling agonies which, for example, an aunt and uncle of mine both suffered twenty-five years ago. In fact it is, generally speaking, only in accidents or the sudden onset of illness that we are today called upon to endure severe physical pain. Once we are under medical care relief is usually at hand. Indeed, we demand it, even in less serious cases. At the dentist, injections are the order of the day for all fillings, and gas for extractions. And to come right down to the pettiest details, the thousands of millions of tablets of aspirin and paracetamol sold annually testify to our unwillingness to put up even with minor discomforts.

The same insistence on freedom from hardship runs through the arrangements of our ordinary daily life. If we can afford it, we keep our houses warm from top to bottom – no getting up or going to bed in cold bedrooms for us. Chairs and beds get ever more comfortable. What a recent change all this is! Unless I am misremembering and making the past a heroic age, my own life as a boy at school and in the army, and even as a young curate, was marked by considerable discomfort which one took for granted, and which gave pleasures when they came a keen edge of delight. Now I live in a luxury which most of the kings buried in this Abbey would have found unbelievable. And millions of us do the same. We must not get side-tracked on to the question whether this is morally good or bad – beyond perhaps reflecting that in our society it is so often those who can least bear these discomforts, the old and the poor, who have to suffer them. What we do need to take to heart is that our civilisation is geared to comfort, that we meet with less physical hardship or distress than any generation that has ever lived, and that our capacity to put up with such distress is also less.

With these things come two other consequences. To our credit, we are concerned that others should not needlesssly suffer the hardships and deprivations from which we have escaped, even if we are apt to leave it to government and institutions to put that concern into practice. But also, to our great loss, we are losing the realistic awareness of what it is to suffer physically, and therefore, worse still, the sense of how vital it is to be ready to suffer in the body in order to keep the soul alive.

In his Rectorial Address to the University of St Andrews in 1922 James Barrie said: 'Courage is the thing. All goes if courage goes.' In the end, the exact measure of how much we care about something – or someone – is how much we are prepared to suffer for their sake. This rule applies whether we are talking about our country, our family, our principles, or our God. No virtue is worth anything at all unless we stick to it when it hurts to do so – and the trouble is, as Jesus said to Peter, James and John in Gethsemane, 'The spirit is eager, but human nature is weak.'

Do we believe in speaking the truth? That will be known when we have done something wrong and confess it fully and accurately, knowing the consequences: when, let us say, we find ourselves in court, charged with an offence which we have in fact committed. Do we plead 'Guilty' or 'Not guilty'? Do we tell all, or do we try to get away with a censored version? Or again, do we believe in being faithful to our wife or husband? The real test comes when, let us say, a woman whose husband has been selfish and indifferent finds understanding and sympathy in another man who is in love with her and she with him; or when a man who is still vigorous but whose wife may have become unresponsive is struck with overwhelming physical attraction for a younger and more beautiful woman who wants him for herself. In such cases the pain of self-restraint can seem unbearable and never-ending. Without real courage, the principle is bound to go by the board.

So it is too with more humdrum things. Being responsible and reliable in our daily duties, going on with what has to be done even though we are depressed or tired, this too calls for courage. You may know these lines from John Masefield's poem, *The Ever-lasting Mercy* —

> 'To get the whole world out of bed
> And washed, and dressed, and warmed, and fed,
> To work, and back to bed again,
> Believe me, Saul, costs worlds of pain.'

In the end, this kind of faithfulness has to be prepared to go the whole way. The ultimate test of how much we care for a principle or a person is whether we are prepared to die for them. Not so long ago we in this country were brutally challenged and critized by Alexander Solzhenitsyn; and the nub of his criticism came down to this – that he doubted whether we were any longer prepared to *die*, if necessary, for freedom against tyranny, for truth against the lie, for justice against oppression. I do not myself think the moral paralysis has gone so fatally far as he believes. I think the trouble is very largely that we cannot bring ourselves to believe that the Russian Communists and their allies are either as evil or as hostile as some declare them to be. Personally I have no doubts at all: the appalling crimes that defile every page of Communist history right up to this very day; the millions of innocent people who have been tortured and killed in defiance of the laws even of Soviet Russia itself, simply for having opinions unacceptable to their rulers; the trouble fomented by Communists in every country outside their empire; their gigantic and ever-growing waste of wealth on armaments of every kind at the expense of their own people and to no justifiable purpose; these undeniable facts convince me. And when we read, as we all very easily can, in such books as Amnesty International's *Prisoners of Conscience in the U.S.S.R.*, or Trevor Beeson's *Discretion and Valour*, or Solzhenitsyn's own books, of the heroic refusal of numbers of men and women to let even that overwhelming machine of tyranny dictate the inner life of their spirit, we surely recognise that there today Christ is still crucified.

In these unconquerable souls, many of them Christians, many not, we see Jesus Christ more clearly in our midst than perhaps anywhere else on earth. They too know, as Jesus did in the garden, the squad with truncheons, the midnight arrest, out of sight of ordinary folk. There are, alas, others, many others carrying the same cross, for evil knows no frontiers. In the political prisons of South America, in Africa – black and white, in Asia, there are Calvaries by the score. And it is right to call them by that glorious name, because the victims share with Jesus this one primary and basic virtue without which love and goodness and human fulfilment can in the end never survive: COURAGE.

To have courage does not prove a man or woman good or in the right. Many villains have been brave. But no one can be really and truly good without it. Jesus said it all when he told his disciples: 'Whosoever will come after me, let him deny himself and take up his cross and follow me. For whosoever will save his life shall lose it; but whosoever shall lose his life for my sake and the Gospel's, the same shall save it. For what shall it profit a man, if he shall gain the whole world, and lose his own soul?' This lesson of courage – 'to teach his brethren and inspire, to suffer and to die' – however terrifying the cost, however rightly our human nature shrinks from it, is the first and most necessary thing we have to take into our hearts and lives from the Cross of Christ.

14

Preached in Westminster Abbey,
on Easter Day 1974.

The Meaning of the Resurrection

'WHY DID I bother?' we say. 'Why did I go to all that trouble? They couldn't stop even for five minutes' – 'They never even noticed the flowers' – 'They couldn't have cared less about my present' – 'Why did I make all those sacrifices to see that they wanted for nothing when they were young? They never come to see me now; perhaps a couple of hours every six months, and you can tell they find it a nuisance.'

Small cruelties, maybe, but what heartbreak! and if such things can break our hearts, what did the rejection of his only Son do to the heart of God? After Good Friday might he not have asked himself, 'Why did I bother?' And if we think he could hardly have been blamed for that, is there not another question, this time one we should be asking ourselves, this Easter morning? Why, after all that, did God trouble himself about us any further?

For the Resurrection need not have happened in the way it did. God could have raised Jesus from the grave in the silence of eternity, and then taken no steps whatever to let us know what he had done. Or he could have allowed us a glimpse of Jesus in a devastating glory that would have said more plainly than any words that we had missed our chance and were doomed to incurable despair.

But he did neither of these things. The Gospels vary widely in their Easter stories, and in many points are, as you would expect, deeply mysterious. But on one thing they are all agreed. Jesus comes to his friends to renew the ties of friendship broken by their failures and his death. His first greeting to the terrified disciples in the Upper Room is, 'Peace be unto you'; it is when he breaks bread with the two at Emmaus that he is recognised by them; in Matthew his last words are, 'Lo, I am with you always, even to the end of the world'; Simon Peter is given the threefold opportunity

57

to reverse his threefold denial.

In the Resurrection God gives Jesus back to the human race; and because he has passed through death, and comes to them now 'in the power of an endless life', this time he is given to them never to be taken away again. The Cross by itself could not assure us of the love of God for us. If the story had ended on Good Friday we would never have known whether God had perhaps ceased to care for his ungrateful children. It is the giving back of Jesus to his own at Easter which tells us that God cares invincibly. And that is why Easter is the crown and completion of the Gospel.

'But wait a minute!' someone will say. 'You're cheating! It sounds very fine to say, "God gives Jesus back to humankind," but it just isn't true. He gave him back to some of his friends and disciples and to no one else. How can you talk as though God gave Jesus back to *me*, or to thousands of millions of other people? In the first place we never knew him (nor did you for that matter), so we didn't reject him and we couldn't lose him; and in the second place, we have never seen him (nor have you), so we haven't had him back!'

The objection is a fair one, indeed it could be put even more strongly. Were even the first disciples so much better off? After all, Jesus did not walk and talk with them for very long. A matter of weeks and they were on their own once more. But it is also quite clear from everything they said and did that they did not feel on their own. There must be something more to it than we have so far described, something which applies equally to us and to them, and which makes Easter a blessing not just to those who saw Jesus in the flesh but also to those 'who have not seen and yet have believed.'

The crucial factor, the thing which decides whether Easter really works for us, is, as it always is in Christianity, the answer we give to the question: 'Who is Jesus?' Was he just a great and good man, or is he also something more – 'God from God, Light from Light, True God from True God, One in Being with the Father'? Easter is for praise not pedantry; and I have no intention of lecturing you on the reasons for believing that Jesus is the eternal Son of God. But what I must try to do is to say in a few words why, if we do believe it, Easter turns the whole of life into praise.

God, you see, *is*, our life. We create, we reproduce ourselves, we shape our own destinies, but in the end the power for all this comes from him. We live only because he upholds us and believes in us. It's rather like the old story of the man who never had any matches, and was always borrowing from a friend when he wanted to light his pipe. One day the friend asked: 'Why do you always use *my* matches? Why can't you get some of your own?' 'All right,' came the reply, 'if that's your attitude, I'll take the box and be independent of you!' In a sense God allows us to take the box, but ultimately it is still his.

But this power of life within us: is it good or evil, kindly or cruel, or just blind and neutral? Left to ourselves we can never be quite sure. Even if we believed in a God, we might at times wonder if he were a devil. But in Jesus all this fear and doubt is done away. God is not some ambiguous cosmic force. He who gives us his life to use has a human face, nay more, the face of a friend and a unique friend, the Man Jesus. In the light of Easter Day we see finally and beyond all question that the divine life within us shares and cares invincibly and for ever.

And does not this change everything? Change it, oh! so infinitely for the better! The first joy of Easter is that our lives, yours and mine, are no longer solitary, hopeless affairs. Each life is a partnership: ourself on the one hand, Christ who upholds us and all the worlds on the other. If we then will but share his values, his love for all creatures, his power and joy have free course in us, and all our fear and fretfulness is done away.

The second joy of Easter is that what is true of us is true of everyone. There is no single person in the whole world who lives and thinks and feels for any other reason than that Christ upholds him and believes in him. When I say, 'Good morning', on the train or over the garden fence, it is not just my neighbour whom I greet. It is also Christ.

And the third joy of Easter is that what is true of men and women is true of all created things. 'Lo, the fair beauty of earth, from the death of the winter arising! Every good gift of the year now with its Master returns.' So the ancient hymn-writer, 1300 years ago. But his words are true in an even deeper sense. With the return of Christ from the grave no creature in the universe can ever be completely hateful or ugly again, since it is he who upholds it and believes in it.

And the fourth joy of Easter is the best of all. The glory that

Easter brings into our lives is a personal thing; it all springs from the fact that a particular person, Jesus the Son of God, has committed himself to each and every one of us without reserve, in order to make us, like himself, sons and daughters of his Father. And is he, who conquered death, going to let death break that bond, frustrate that commitment? Of course not! 'Christ, being raised from the dead, dieth no more; death hath no more dominion over him.' And when the time comes, he who has shared every moment of your life and mine, will guide us along the path that he too has trodden; and 'the darkness will be no darkness with him, but the night will be as clear as the day.'

15 Dreaming the Right Dreams

So also is the resurrection of the dead. It is sown in
corruption; it is raised in incorruption: it is sown
in dishonour; it is raised in glory: it is sown in
weakness; it is raised in power.
1 Corinthians 15. 42–43

HOW MANY PEOPLE today, who would sincerely call themselves
Christians, have lost, or more probably never had, one great
thing which used to be a distinguishing mark of Christians? I
mean a positive joy and confidence in the face of death. Not just
the capacity to master our natural human shrinking from death,
an assurance of something beyond, but a burning, inspiring conviction that what is to come is better than what we have known
here. Our life now tends moment by moment toward that which
Saint Paul described as corruption, dishonour, weakness. Do we
truly and honestly see beyond that the new existence of incorruption, glory, power of which he speaks? As he puts it in another
place: 'I think that the sufferings of this present time are not
worthy to be compared with the glory that shall be revealed *in*
us.' Note that he says, 'in us', not 'to us'. One of the signs of God's
own glory in the age to come is what he will make of us.

Anyone who has been chronically ill or weak or crippled will
appreciate what that means. As the well-known hymn puts it: 'O
how glorious and resplendent fragile body shalt thou be! When
endued with so much beauty, full of health and strong and free.
Full of vigour, full of pleasure, that shall last eternally.' But how
often, I wonder, do we think of that, or tell it to others, when accident or disease strike, and life closes in upon us. Mostly it never
occurs to us to do so, for there is nothing solid or real about our
idea of the life to come.

But even if we did think of eternal life in that way it would be
only half the story. For our Christian hope is that heaven is not

61

just compensation for bad times undergone here but also fulfilment of joy and goodness that begin here. Our faith is that what is to come is better, not than the worst life has to offer – that would be little indeed, but better than life's very best. Yet not by replacing the best we know with something utterly different but by fulfilling it. There the beauty so often glimpsed and gone will not only surround us but shine from us. There the great song of which we have caught but the tantalising echoes we shall not only hear but sing. We forget, to our own incalculable loss we forget, but it is the very heart of the Good News of Jesus Christ, that God his Father, the God of the Resurrection, is a God of dreams come true – nay more, that our dreams are true, they are given us as messengers of the truth. In the words of Abelard's incomparable hymn:

> 'Jerusalem is the city
> of everlasting peace,
> a peace that is surpassing
> and utter blessedness;
> where finds the dreamer waking
> truth beyond dreaming far,
> nor is the heart's possessing
> less than the heart's desire.'[1]

But if there is this continuity between our dreams here and our waking in eternity, then, as both Paul and John insist, eternal life has already begun, and our resurrection will be just a logical climax to our life on earth. 'He that believes on me *has* eternal life, and I will raise him up at the last day.' Is it not rather stupid and wishful thinking to talk like that? Indeed it can be if our dreams are false and unworthy ones. You might say that the most important business of all our lives is to dream the right dreams. If you want to know what these are, you can of course go to the Jesus of the Gospels, or to some other great master of the good life and read what they have to say. But perhaps we can work out some of them for ourselves, simply by experience. After all, what we find out that way always means more and sticks longer than what we are told by others.

If there are traces of eternal life in our lives here and now, then obviously we are not going to find them in those things that fade and pass away even during our brief time on earth. It is no use my

[1] The translation is that by Helen Waddell in *Mediaeval Latin Lyrics*.

expecting to row stroke any more in a racing eight; nor can you, madam, charming though you are, still expect the young men's stomachs to turn over and their hearts to pound as once they did. Nor will we look, if we have any sense, for traces of eternity in things which mere chance can take away at any time: money, for instance, or power. If we are to be able to say, 'Grow old along with me, the best is yet to be,' then we must look for the things that get better and stronger as life goes on; and that means essentially the things of the spirit.

Is this not truly how we all find it? Our senses may not be so vibrant and overwhelming as they were in childhood and youth; but our appreciation, our powers of objective observation are deeper. Life may not be quite so jolly and free as it was at twenty-one, but our understanding is infinitely greater, both of others and of ourselves. We have learned, pray God, to forgive more readily, to be compassionate not just with those who easily excite anyone's sympathy, but with the difficult and off-putting. We cannot have everything we want, but we value more what we have, and especially love and friendship. We cannot do everything we would like, but our interest and concern can go on growing wider and livelier. We have seen through the myth of independence, and now cherish belonging. We are not bowled over by setbacks as once we were, but paradoxically hope more steadily when to all seeming there is less time for hope. And with all this comes a beauty and tranquillity and depth of resource far richer than mere gorgeousness or good spirits or energy. It is in fact a strength and beauty that our appearance and our bodies can never do justice to but only hint at. But when those bodies are renewed, glorified, then it is this inner strength and beauty that they will express and express perfectly, just as Jesus's risen body expressed him, with all his love, compassion, understanding and strength.

As Paul said: 'It is sown a natural body, it is raised a spiritual body.' And the glory that shines through the spiritual body is God's glory precisely because these good things, these eternal things which have grown stronger while all else was fading and weakening, are reflections of God's own heart as we have learned to see this in Jesus.

But of course that glory will not shine through us if we have used our time to move away from it into darkness, or to cherish those things that can never endure. How many men cling to a false youth, struggling to keep up some futile ideal of athletic prowess, boasting of what they did in their prime! How many women cannot bear the thought of encroaching years, and waste money and time on a quest for a kind of beauty that can no longer be theirs and which can never conceal the discontent within them! How many of both sexes become more dependent on possessions, acquiring more things as the time and opportunity for using and enjoying them grows less! And these are but the most obvious follies. The kind of questions we need to ask ourselves as life moves on are these: Where we ought to have deeper understanding, is there merely cynicism, a 'seeing through it all', or grudges and resentment? Where there should be a more sensitive compassion, do we find the attitude, 'Oh, I've no patience with people like that!'? Where there should be a greater value set on belonging, on the possibilities of love and friendship, are we falling into the trap of family feuds and petty jealousies? The more we have had out of life, the more ready we should be to make sacrifices for others; but how often is this so? Nor are these the failings of old age only. They begin to get a hold upon us quite young, in our forties especially, when we feel that the halfway mark of life is past and are tempted to self-pity. And the more we give way to such things, the less capable we become of grasping our true hope. For those who are immersed in wrong values in this life become less and less able to catch even a glimpse of the life beyond, and their ears grow deaf to the snatches of its songs.

In the book of Exodus there is a story of the children of Israel which is a kind of parable of this earthly condition of ours. There they are, halfway between deliverance and promise, between their miraculous escape from Egypt and the land flowing with milk and honey. But for the moment they are in the wilderness. The past no longer gives them confidence, the future no longer inspires hope. So they turn for consolation to the solid things they can touch and see. They make them gods of gold; they sit down to eat and drink and rise up to play.

We too are in the wilderness of this world. The Easter miracle of our redemption, the Cross and Resurrection, is so far in the past; 'the mist of doubt, the blight of love's decay' has made the future problematic. As individuals, as a nation, as a church even, seized with some terrible self-destructive madness we turn to the gods of gold, and few are those who voluntarily embrace simplicity of life in order to help others and to give the tender grass of the spirit a chance to grow. Let us ask ourselves, each one of us, where we stand on this. It is not just an issue of our society and its survival. It could be, for each one of us, the issue of eternal life. For it is still true today, and always will be, that it is the things that are seen which are temporal and pass away, but the things that are not seen which are eternal.

16 The Duties of the State

Preached in St Margaret's, Westminster,
29 April 1979.

*'Render unto Caesar the things that are Caesar's,
and unto God the things that are God's.'*
St Matthew 22.21

THE POINT THAT Jesus did not deal with in this saying is whether there is anything that Caesar has to render to God. On the face of it the words mean that government as such is a part of the divine order – God does not back anarchy, he has made us creatures who need social organisation and a settled framework of conventions and ways of doing things, common policies for achieving objectives of importance to all. They also mean that people have a duty to support the government under which they live, to pay their taxes, and so on. This was said of a pagan government and Jesus's followers took it at its face value. There is no support here for the idea that we should obey or co-operate with only a government of whose theories and policies we approve.

Equally, however, the early Christians did eventually disobey the Roman government when it pushed them too far. They would not do anything to compromise their religious beliefs, chiefly by venerating the Emperor as divine. This was a matter of rendering to God alone the thing that was peculiarly his, namely worship.

But, of course, in the circumstances it was not quite right to describe this as a purely religious matter. Roman society, the huge sprawling Empire, was held together by this religious act, for some superstitious, for others almost mystical. Worship of the Emperor's image expressed a belief that loyalty to Rome was an ultimate duty, that the Empire was part of the eternal order, a divinely ordained structure of human life. To refuse that worship was to subvert the very foundations of human life, the way everything not only was but ought to be organised. It was as dangerous as a barbarian invasion. And when the pagans blamed Christian defiance in this matter for the fact that the barbarians did

66

invade, and the Empire collapsed in ruins, they showed a deeper intuition about the significance of what Christians had done than the Christians themselves, who insisted that it was simply a question of individual conscience. The political vision of Christian thinkers in the last centuries of the Roman Empire had developed in a quite distinctive way. They had built up the idea of the Church as almost a nation within a nation, as an alternative kingdom with its own people and princes, but a kingdom that would survive when the world came to its soon and destined end. The glory of the secular, pagan world was the glory promised by Satan to Jesus in the wilderness, a glory founded on pride, riches, lust and tyranny, as opposed to the glory of the Christian people, marked by humility, poverty, simplicity of life, generosity to the poor, purity, self-control, brotherhood and freedom. Having made this particular analysis of the human situation, the leaders of the Church could face the collapse of the Empire, if not without apprehension, at least with some detachment and long-term assurance. No one was more deeply wedded in his heart to the great system and culture of Rome than St Augustine; but as the Vandals drew ever nearer to North Africa, moving south through Spain, he exorcised his fears, and tried to assuage those of his flock, by writing his greatest work *The City of God*, on the theme 'Two loves have built two cities' – and only the one built by love for God would in the end survive.

It is often said that what destroyed the soul of Christianity was its alliance with the State after Constantine made it the official religion of the Empire. This did, it is true, bring into the Church many nominal Christians, with all the fudging of commitment and standards one might expect; and in the Eastern Mediterranean it did lead to a close identification of Church and State. But not in Western Europe. When St Augustine wrote, the Empire had been officially Christian for more than a hundred years; but that still did not lead him to equate the life of this world with the Kingdom of God. On the contrary, he gave classic and influential form to their separation. And despite efforts to bring them together at the Reformation and since, the dominant view in Western Europe has always been that the spheres of Church and State have been essentially distinct. Men and women take care for their eternal destiny by sharing the faith, worship and personal conduct of the Church, and so, if they are wise, sit light to the world. But that world goes on by its own rules; and if it is harsh or unjust the Christian as an individual simply has to endure it. In seventeenth century Anglicanism the 'Doctrine of the Cross' was seen supremely in the duty of passive obedience to the worst of rulers.

In modern times we have moved slowly away from this position, first, to assert the right of Christians, never entirely abandoned, to criticise society and government in the light of God's moral law, and then, most recently, to argue that Christians can, in extreme cases, rightly join in violent resistance and rebellion to change political systems that are deaf to the pleas of justice or mercy.

The latter point is too complex to argue now. It is tied up with the whole question of Christian attitudes to war, which is agonisingly difficult. As regards the former, I suppose, we would all want to say that Christians are bound from their own standpoint to criticise the State, and have every right to do so, as much as the adherents of any other faith or philosophy. Which brings me back to the question I asked at the beginning: What must Caesar render to God? It is not enough to divide life into two areas, God and the State, with the individual trying to do his or her duty by each. The individual cannot render to God the things that are God's unless the State makes it possible to do so, or at least does not make it impossible. At the heart of our Lord's command is an assumption that Caesar will respect his proper limits and do his basic duties.

Another way of putting this is to say that one of the great responsibilities of Government is to make it as easy as possible for people to be good, that is, to live as God intends. Now, our criticism of Caesar on this basis will obviously be determined by what we think God does intend, what a good life is. Also, we must ask, is 'making it easy for people to be good' the same, in some cases, as 'making it difficult to be bad'? We have, for example, the task, as Christians, of making up our mind about such moral issues as abortion, divorce, euthanasia, pornography, and so forth; but we also have to decide whether the law should come down severely on those who take a different view. If tolerance is a virtue necessary for a free, civilised society, when does it come second to protecting the young, the ignorant, the weak, the psychologically vulnerable?

The Duties of the State

Or again, what do you do about those who exploit the creed of tolerance in order to have a riot for their own sinister ends? No doubt the best response to the National Front would be to ostracise them, to let them march down empty streets past blank windows. But some are sincerely too angered to do that, and others see a grand opportunity to provoke the police and damage just a little more the idea of a disciplined but free society. What do we as Christians think should be done about that? Anyone can condemn the National Front. That's easy. It is a lot harder to come up with a Christian answer to the other, resultant problem, which is just as great a danger if not greater. Do our beliefs about the deep sinfulness of human nature, as well as its goodness, and about the need to keep little ones from stumbling, have anything to say to us here?

Often, too, we are told that a Christian may have views about the goals of politics – quality of life, caring for the weak, freedom, responsibility, fair shares, and so on – but not about the technical means of trying to achieve them. There is a fallacy here too easily overlooked. On such general matters most people are against sin and in favour or virtue. The real argument is about how you put this into practice. And here there must be Christian views simply because different approaches have different merits and demerits. Take that political cliché, the 'caring society'. We all want one. For either side to denounce the other as uncaring gets us nowhere. The argument is about how you create a caring society. Do you expect most of the caring to be done by State money and action, or do you put more responsibility on the citizen and try to create a situation in which it is more practicable, for example, for people to care for their own families, old folk and so forth? It is just not true that one view is Christian, the other non-Christian; there are good Christian arguments for both, and in practice we need a mix of the two. Or take education: some Christians see independent education as socially divisive and an unfair privilege of the affluent, and oppose it on those grounds. Others, such as myself, find it intolerably dangerous that all education should by law be in the hands of the State, and could never vote for a party that wanted to give the State that much power over people's minds. But one does not therefore dismiss the other people as un-Christian. We need to learn from each other: independent education ought to be available to the poor, State

69

education ought to be genuinely open to all wisdom including religious faith. Both objectives are hard to achieve, but achieving them is what Christian politics is about. Both views are Christian views because they are arrived at by thinking on Christian lines. But if so, then, what all Christians must surely be vigilant and tireless in opposing is anything at all that might move society in the direction of a one-party State, and so render to Caesar that kingdom and power and glory which belongs to God alone.

17 Memories

FROM TIME TO time some poor soul is found wandering by the police, and taken to hospital suffering from loss of memory. Often this loss is quite limited, and covers only the hours or days just past. The patient knows who he is and where he comes from, but has no idea how he came to be, let us say, in Victoria Street when he actually lives in Macclesfield. But sometimes there is a general loss of memory; and then the victim cannot recall his name or his job or his home, whether he has a wife and family, how old he is – anything. Even the clothes he is wearing. And this is a terrifying situation to be in. For what are we without our memory? Our whole character, the personality we have built up over the years is made out of memories. To have no memories is to become a ghost.

As we grow older, memories play a larger and larger part in our lives. There is not much we can do now to change the general shape of our story. There are fewer things we can expect to achieve. What we have to offer depends much more on the sort of people we are; and the sort of person we are is very much a matter of how we think and feel about the past – what we have done, the people we have known, the cards life has dealt to us. As the years slip by, nothing is more important than that we should do our remembering in the right spirit.

Take first the memory of the good things in our lives. All too often it happens that when people get to the age at which they need more physical comfort, they have a rougher time of it than ever before; when they need security they are worried sick about money; when they need company they are left alone. In such circumstances how do we use the memory of happier days? In a well-known line Tennyson once wrote: 'This is truth the poet sings, that a sorrow's crown of sorrow is remembering happier things.' Does it always have to be that way? We can understand only too well that it might be so. We look back to the time when, perhaps, we were people of some consequence, or had a good income, or a large family around us, and we feel bitter or resentful and ready to give up. It must be hard not to do that; yet we all know people who don't fall into that trap. Their happy memories give them courage and comfort; they love to think with gratitude of all the blessings they have enjoyed, and actually find their hardships easier to bear because of their memories.

Again, in bereavement we all know that at first memories of happiness shared bring the tears more than almost anything else. A photograph of somewhere we spent that wonderful day, the flowers we planted together, the music we loved to listen to, all break our hearts. But after a time we can bear to think of these things, and it is good to remember how much happiness there was. Sometimes, indeed, it is only after the other has gone that we realise how much there was. At the time we used to fuss and grumble so, that we hardly noticed the deep inner contentment we shared with them. There is a lesson here: Remember the good things. Remember them as they happen, day by day. Be grateful for them as they go by. Then later on they will be a strength and consolation. It is because we remember the 'pastures green' and the 'quiet waters' that we are aware of God's rod and staff comforting us even in the darkest valley.

But, of course and alas, there are also bad things that haunt our remembrance. And here I am thinking not so much of grief and pain. These leave their mark, indeed; and there is a kind of quiet shadow behind the eyes of those who have suffered long and grievously which never quite lifts even in the midst of laughter. But much more difficult to cope with, I believe, are the black passages of shame and remorse. How we failed to be patient, to give sympathy or understanding; how cruel we were with our tongue; the dirty trick we played to cheat someone of what was rightfully theirs; the grudge we bore for real or imagined wrongs ... and still do bear? How do we deal with memories like that?

So often we alter the story, we tell and re-tell it to ourselves and to others, gradually whitewashing our own part and finding reasons to put the blame on someone else. Perhaps we made a real hash of some part of our life, ended up in prison, lost a good job, broke up a marriage; and memory works away finding excuses and reasons, putting things in a different light, so that we can sleep more easily. Not that we do, even then. In the end we just push the whole business away, and never allow ourselves or anyone else to refer to it. But this is all wrong. For it is just as important to remember the bad things, and to remember them honestly and accurately, to face the truth about ourselves and others. If we do not we shall never know nor give happiness.

Few of us can look back and not say with John Henry Newman in the words of that famous hymn, 'Pride ruled my will'. If we want peace at the end of a lifetime we must forgive and be forgiven. No one can go through a human life and not make mistakes, do selfish and regrettable things. But we can learn from these memories: we can learn our own need for forgiveness, and make up our minds to seek it right away. We can admit our faults to God and say we are sorry; and God will forgive us. But to know the fullest peace and happiness we need to admit our faults to our fellow-men and women as well, to say 'Sorry' to those we have treated badly. We need to try and mend that stupid family feud, not by lecturing others, but by just admitting our own share and apologising. We need to be humble, hard though it is, toward the child who left home and has never been back. We may not succeed in putting things right; it may be an outside chance. But it is the only chance, and they will never be put right if we don't try. And if we refuse to remember things as they really were, obviously they never will, and many lives may be spoiled.

The other advantage of remembering truthfully is that it helps us to do for others what in later life we are best at: and that is passing on help and encouragement and wisdom. How often we older people (and this sets in very early) go on about the young, quite forgetting what we ourselves were really like! We complain, maybe, that they are irresponsible about money or jobs or keeping their word: but were we so wonderful at that age? We say they waste their opportunities at college, chances we never had, but if we had their heads on our shoulders, would we do any better? We think them permissive, perhaps, and forget how one feels, how silly (in our eyes, now) we all were about girls and boys. Now when the young get in a jam, they need help, and they will take notice, provided it is honest. And we can give that help so long as we remember what life was really like and do not clothe ourselves with a good sense and holiness we never possessed. Remember your own life steadily and whole, and you will always have something worthwhile to contribute to the life of those around you.

Before Jesus ascended into heaven he told us to do something 'in remembrance' of him. And the way we remember Jesus is a pattern and parable of the vital part memory plays in our whole life. We remember all that he did and suffered for us, his teaching, the healing of the sick, the forgiveness he brought to us from God for all the sins and cruelties of men, including our own; we remember the past with honesty and thankfulness. And the memory of all these things gives us strength and comfort in the present; it brings that 'power from on high' in which we try to help others. But the memory of Jesus's ascension to glory convinces us of something even more wonderful: that the future, too, belongs to God; that one day we shall hear him say 'Yet there is room, there is room at my side for thee'; that where he is we shall be also; that nothing that is good can ever be lost; and that the time will come when what are now for us just cherished memories will once more be realities, when we and those we love are reunited in the glory of eternal life.

18

Preached in Westminster Abbey on Rogation Sunday,
23 May 1976.

Listening to God

MOST OF US, if we pray at all, will at some time have wondered, 'Am I just talking to myself?' If our faith is a bit shaky (and my own often goes through phases when I think that perhaps we have all been kidding ourselves, and there is in fact no God) then one cannot help feeling how helpful it would be if the conversation we call prayer were not so very one-sided. And even those whose faith is strong find at times a longing for some actual word or sign that God is there and listening.

In the lives of Christians who have been great men and women of prayer we do, it is true, hear frequently of God speaking to them through an inner voice, bringing light and strength in their perplexities, or giving a new vision and conviction. Some of the most famous sayings of Christian history have come to us from this source: Mother Julian's, 'All shall be well, and all manner thing shall be well'; Teresa of Avila's complaint to our Lord about the appalling hardships of a January journey through flooded country to Burgos, when our Lord replied, 'But that is how I treat my friends,' and received the famous retort from the saint, 'Then, Lord, no wonder you have so few'; or Thomas Aquinas, who in prayer heard Jesus offering him any reward he chose for all the work he had done to uphold the faith, and replied *Non nisi te*, 'None except thyself.' Or again, to come to modern times and more ordinary examples, I know someone who had been praying in church and it seemed to them that the crucifix on the altar said (or, at any rate, that the words which formed themselves in the mind seemed to originate from it), 'You will make no headway in converting the world until my Church is one.'

I mention these stories for two reasons. First, to point out that even when people do receive a word or sign in prayer this does not prove anything in the way we sometimes wish for proof. Even if God does speak to us, there is no way in which he can do so which can possibly prove beyond all doubt that it is God speaking. For us to recognise him as God he would have to say the kind of thing

75

or, in the case of a vision, put on the kind of appearance which we associate with God. And if he does that, then, of course, it can always be argued that the words or the vision came out of our own heads. They were just what we were conditioned to hear or see. So, if our faith needs stiffening, that is not going to help very much.

But the second reason for telling the stories is to remind us that what people do receive in this way in prayer is very much what they as individuals are capable of receiving. Such experiences express what is already there deep down in the personality. Teresa of Avila showed in her whole life that in hardship and disappointment she saw an opportunity to live closer to Christ. So it is not surprising that when, under great strain, her exasperation burst out in her prayers she should hear Jesus crystallise in memorable words what was the innermost heart of her own existence: 'That is how I treat my friends.' But it is when we appreciate that this was what she most profoundly believed, so profoundly in fact that it could be voiced unconsciously in this way, that we see the real spiritual significance of her famous reply. Only someone who was quite unshakably wedded to God, and wrapped up in him, could spontaneously adopt that tone of humorous irritation on such a subject: 'No wonder you have so few.' Giovanni Guareschi made the point very well when, in a preface to one of the last Don Camillo books, he said that the voice from the Cross in those stories was best thought of as coming from the deepest levels of Don Camillo's own conscience.

Am I saying, then, that any light and guidance we receive in prayer are nothing more than our own unconscious selves? Certainly not. To put the question that way is to misunderstand the situation. What we receive in prayer comes *through* ourselves; but it comes *from* the interaction between ourselves and God, and what that has made of us. Perhaps an imaginary human situation may make things clearer.

Let us suppose that we have a sticky personal problem, at work, perhaps, or in the family. We are fed up, we simply must let off steam to someone, get help or advice or anyway sympathy. Whom shall we try? (Forgive me if I tell this story from a man's angle; I think the characters could all be transformed into women without affecting the basic principle, even if the details would be different.) Well, obviously someone who is a good liste-

ner. Not Smith, who is always just off somewhere to an urgent
appointment, nor Jones, who keeps tapping his fingernails on
the arm of his chair, and saying, 'Yes, yes', in the most blatantly
bored and irritated manner. Of course, Robinson, just the man!
Kindness itself, always delighted to see you. We go round to
Robinson. He is in; in no time coffee is produced, or something
stronger, and we are away. Nor does he let us down. He expresses
shock and disgust, sympathy and encouragement, at all the
proper places. Two hours later we go away – comforted? heart-
ened? Well, not really, and certainly not for long. In fact, if it were
not ungrateful we would say that we felt rather flat, dissatisfied
with something we know not what. Over the next few days we
realise that Robinson has not helped one little bit.

So, since the problem refuses to go away, we try again. We
decide to talk to Brown. He too is a kindly soul and a good listener,
but we are all the same slightly nervous. We are just a little in
awe of him, as we could never be of Robinson, because it is only too
certain that Brown would never have got himself into the kind of
mess we are in. Now, you know as well as I do what happens when
we try to unfold our tale to him. It sounds quite different. All
those things we said which seemed so justified at the time, were
they not rather cheap, perhaps, or cowardly, or even cruel? We
keep thinking of things we failed to do, which we obviously ought
to have tried, or of ways in which we could have been more reasonable or imaginative. Our story is punctuated by ever more frequent pauses, and by comments such as, 'I suppose I should
have . . .', or, 'I don't think I really . . .' Finally we start questioning our whole attitude. Perhaps what we wanted all along was
wrong, perhaps it was our values that were upside down. By the
time we have unravelled the whole sorry tangle it does not much
matter what Brown says. Just because he is the kind of person he
is, a real change has already taken place inside ourselves.

And as with our friends, so surely with God and Jesus – or so
surely it ought to be. God does not have to 'say' anything in the
crude and obvious sense. The fact that it is him we are talking to
causes us ourselves to say what needs to be said, and to say it in
the most effective way, drawing up from the depths of our being
convictions we never knew we had.

The same transforming effect applies to all our prayer, not just
to our reflection on our failures, sins and shortcomings, or our

perplexities about what to do for the best. It affects all our asking. To take one obvious example. We follow a Master who healed the sick both in body and mind. But we follow him also in trusting a Father who spared not his own Son from suffering and death. It is wholly right that we should lay before God our griefs and anxieties for those we love and for ourselves; and experience shows that doing so does again and again bring restoration or new resources. But if we know who it is to whom we speak, and what he himself found it right to endure, we shall not presume in advance what specific blessing is to come. We shall ask for what we want – certainly we shall, for we must always be honest with God. But we shall ask in a Gethsemane way, trusting him to give some better thing than what we have, but not knowing what that better thing is necessarily to be. How very wise and how deeply Christian in this respect is the inspired wording of the prayer for 'all sorts and conditions of men' in the Prayer Book, when it asks 'that it may please thee to comfort and relieve them according to their several necessities, giving them patience under their sufferings, and a happy issue out of all their afflictions.'

For that 'happy issue', happy for them and for all those bound up with them in the bundle of life, we can pray in trust and confidence. But only if in our prayer we are talking not to ourselves but to the God who listens, and who has made himself known to us in his world and in his Son. If we never bother to learn what God is like, to think about him and attach our hearts to him, then it will not be he with whom we speak but a fantasy, and we shall indeed end up talking to ourselves. And if we ask then, no wonder if we do not receive, for what can a fantasy give?

19

Preached in the chapel of the Pusey House, Oxford,
on Whit-Sunday 1976.

The Lord and Giver of Life

*'If anyone loves me he will keep my word, and my
Father will love him, and we shall come to him and
make our home with him'. St John 14.23*

A LONG TIME ago, when I was in Oxford, people used to take an
examination known as the Final Honours School of Theology.
This was a somewhat abstruse interrogation on the finer theoretical points of the Christian religion. The whole notion of giving a
degree in such a subject must, of course, seem laughable today,
when anyone interested in such things takes the Joint Honours
School of Sociology and Atheism, which is so much more relevant. But even in those days the arcane and ancient jargon of the
questions did from time to time touch some living concern of the
human soul.

One such question was a favourite old warhorse. In the Old
Testament and Apocrypha there is a good deal about wisdom,
human and divine. Some writers speak of the divine wisdom in a
rather impersonal way, as simply a quality of God, shining forth
from him like the light. Others describe it as an independent personal being – a woman, beautiful, charming and intelligent –
who is a kind of heavenly adviser and assistant to God in all his
works, but who also has a soft spot for the human race and likes to
help them. The question we were asked to decide was, in effect,
whether the writers really thought of divine wisdom as an independent being distinguishable from God himself, or not. Obviously there was no answer to it, but that did not matter. It was a
chance to show knowledge, which is after all not a bad way to set
an examination paper.

You may wonder why I say that this question touched on a
living concern of the human soul. To see how it does so, we have, I
think, to ask ourselves another question: Why did these men talk
of wisdom in this way? why did they swing backwards and for-

wards, unable to choose between two such different images, the impersonal light and the personal mediator between God and Man, impelled, so it would seem, to keep and even rather absurdly to mix the two? And the answer to that takes us right into the heart of our human predicament.

The world God made is a wonderful one, but it is also difficult and baffling, of enormous complexity and mystery. We ourselves are by no means the least complex and mysterious things in it. How to be truly human in this world, how to fulfil our proper role and do what is best for ourselves and all those other creatures who are affected by what we do – that is the jackpot question for the human race now, as it was in biblical times. Only now it has become even more urgent, because we see the possibility, through our intelligence and our technology, of doing ever more and more horrific damage and finally bringing the pillars of the house of life down on top of ourselves and of everything else on this planet. Since God has given this responsibility into our hands, we need minds and hearts to match the responsibility. But that means minds and hearts which have something of the insight and stature of God himself. He knows how our situation should be handled, for he created it. If we could catch just something of that knowledge and capacity we could be inspired rather than crushed by our awesome independence. We need the divine wisdom, just a little of it.

'Where shall wisdom be found?' asks the Book of Job, 'and where is the place of understanding?' And goes on to reply: 'God understandeth the way thereof . . .' Where can we hope to find, receive divine wisdom except from and with the divine? Somehow we must live with God, listen to him day in and day out, go to his tutorials, face his criticisms, be transformed by his personal friendship. The Old Testament writers knew this. But they also knew something else. That no man or woman can hope to do this and live.

This is something that our generation perhaps finds hard to take seriously. Our imaginations, demoralised by the scientific age and its eyes of flesh, have lost touch with the overwhelming majesty of the Lord of Hosts who takes up the isles as a very little thing, the enthroned Judge before whose face heaven and earth flee away. We find God perforce in the quietude of our own inner life and in the intimacy of personal relationships. 'God is Love' means much to us; but correspondingly we forget that both terms of that equation carry a depth of meaning, that it takes its power from the fact that *God*, with all that that means, is Love. And so we think wrongly that we could endure God, that nothing could be easier or more enjoyable than to be on intimate terms with him. And we are oh! so wrong.

Our real dilemma is precisely that we need God but that we cannot endure him. We can live neither with him nor without him. The wise men of the Old Testament knew this and they used their imagery to express it exactly. They dreamed of a divine wisdom which would indeed be truly divine, like the impersonal radiance of his glory, but which would come to Man in a form which he could tolerate and make his own, the gentle, personal friend who is like one of ourselves.

This dream the Gospel proclaims as actuality. 'The Word was made flesh and dwelt among us'; the One who is 'the effulgence of God's glory and the very image of his substance, . . . since . . . the children are sharers in flesh and blood, . . . also himself in like manner partook of the same.' 'No man has seen God at any time; the only-begotten that is in the bosom of the Father, he has made him known'. And made him known not just to give us abstract information about ultimate reality, but because to know the character of God is to have both motive and insight into how to live as a human being. It is to love God's world and to fit into it. And God achieves this by becoming one of us and sharing the life we have to live. How else, after all, did we think it could be done?

But what was done then is not exactly what we have to do now. The world of Jesus recedes from us with increasing velocity. Where is the divine wisdom for today? One possible solution might have been a series of Incarnations, of Boddhisatvas, suited to each great epoch in human affairs. There has been no shortage of candidates. In modern times think of the unimaginably banal Baha'ullah, or more recently the opulent Myung Sung Moon. The trouble with all new Messiahs is that they so obviously fail to live up to the standards set by the first one. For, odd and unlikely though it is, Jesus, who by all the laws of cultural relativism and historical change, ought to mean less and less to fewer and fewer people, in fact strikes more and more in each new generation and in ever new cultures and societies as the One who has the words of life. It is not that the words or the actions recorded of Jesus mean to us now precisely what they meant to those who heard or saw them in the beginning. Obviously they do not. But they have this apparently inexhaustible power to stimulate men and women to the same type and style of life in their own day and circumstances. In other words it is not the letter but the Spirit of Jesus which creates in our hearts a living and relevant wisdom.

And the Spirit of Jesus makes not only Jesus a vital and contemporary presence but also his Father. For as we slowly come to see with the eyes of Jesus and to feel with his heart we begin to know the Father as he knew him. We live in the world as God's world and among men and women as his children; we love the world as God's world and men and women as his children. And that is when the Kingdom of God draws near, is among us, within us.

That then is God the Holy Spirit: God in his contemporary presence. Not a substitute for the Father and the Son. Not just another phase, in which God who once was known as Father and then as Jesus is now to be thought of as something else. God the Holy Spirit is God in his fulness, making both the Father and the Son real to us, Lords both of the world around us and of our hearts within, where they come and make their home. Through Him the Father and the Son say new things to us and we to them. Through Him we learn to cry Abba, Father, and mean it; to say Jesus is Lord, and to mean it. And so long as you can say these things, and mean them in terms of the real life you have to live, then, believe me, it does not matter one jot or tittle whether you say them in tongues. Your life will speak to each man in his own language of the wonderful works of God.

And here in this Eucharist it is the Spirit who moves our hearts to approach the Father with the words of the self-offering of the Son and to know that we are accepted in so doing. There is no lesson that Christian experience teaches more precious than this: that when we truly pour out the words of the Thanksgiving not to ourselves or each other but to the Father, then the Spirit himself bears witness with our spirit that we all, individually and collectively, are children of God. And when that ecstasy of love and joy and gratitude carries out into each living day, so that the world becomes the altar, and everything we do and suffer, every person we meet, becomes the sacrament, then indeed we

The Lord and Giver of Life

begin to know the meaning of the word LIFE.

> Love of the Father, Love of God the Son,
> From whom all came, in whom was all begun,
> Who formest heavenly beauty out of strife,
> Creation's whole desire and breath of life.
>
> Thou the all-holy, thou supreme in might,
> Thou dost give peace, thy presence maketh right;
> Thou with thy favour all things dost enfold,
> With thine all-kindness free from harm wilt hold.
>
> Hope of all comfort, splendour of all aid,
> That does not fail nor leave the heart afraid:
> To all that cry thou dost all help accord,
> The Angels' armour and the Saints' reward.
>
> Eternal glory, all men Thee adore,
> Who art and shalt be worshipped evermore:
> Us whom thou madest, comfort with thy might,
> And lead us to enjoy the heavenly light.

To Whom with the Father and the Son be all glory, all praise and all love in Time and in Eternity. Amen.

20 The Heart of God

Preached in Westminster Abbey,
on Trinity Sunday 1978.

*For love is of God; and every one that loveth is born
of God and knoweth God ... God is love; and he
that dwelleth in love dwelleth in God, and God in
him.' 1 John 4, 7, 16*

MY FIRST JOB after I was ordained was a joint appointment as
curate of a small country parish and very junior lecturer at the
college where I had trained for the ministry. Before each term the
staff came together for a Quiet Day – nothing very elaborate; we
said our Offices and took Holy Communion together, and spent
the rest of our time in silence, reading and praying. At meals we
each brought in a suitable book to read. I remember being somewhat daunted by the standard my senior colleagues set in this
matter: lives of great saints, bishops or theologians; lectures on
science and religion; treatises on prayer. But instead of following their example, I'm sorry to say that I cast my eyes along the
library shelves for a book that would upstage them all; and one
day, tucked away on a top shelf, I found it. It wasn't a big book.
The contents were not all that exciting. But its outside was
impeccable. It had a plain red cover with absolutely nothing
printed on it, no author's or publisher's name or anything except
that on the spine, in gold, it had one word: GOD. I bore it off in
high spirits, and next morning propped it up against the marma-
lade with gratifying effect.

Little things please little minds, alas! But there is a moral in
this childish tale. Theology nowadays concerns itself with many
things: we have theology of sex, theology of race, theology of
work, political theology, theology of revolution, theology of liberation. Even within the sober confines of our university faculties
or in clergy training colleges the subject covers an enormous
range: the languages, thought and cultures of the ancient world;
history; sociology, psychology, philosophy; and the comparative
study of religions. The item which perhaps gets least attention is

the one from which theology takes its name: GOD. Theology means 'the science of God' – but how much does anyone try to say about him?

This is very strange. It is Christianity which claims to have a knowledge of God more certain and intimate than that of any other faith, because it has seen him revealed in Jesus. You would think that Christians would have more than other people to say about God, not less.

There are various reasons for this. One is fairly obvious. Jesus and his teaching as an ideal for human life came to occupy the centre of the stage, so that less thought was given to applying the features of Jesus's character to our picture of God. Today, when belief in God does not come easily, at least to people in the West, there is even more pressure to treat the social and ethical aspects of Jesus as all of permanent significance that he has to give.

But another reason is more deep-seated; and it is ignored because it carries a threat to the whole structure of the Christian faith as we have inherited it. If Jesus is indeed a true revelation of what God is like, of God's methods, character and principles, then a very large part of the picture of God in the Bible has to go. God cannot, for example, be at one and the same time the sort of Person who submits to crucifixion and forgives his enemies, and someone who smites his foes until they come crawling to him in homage. And the same discrepancy runs right through into the picture of eternity. For after we are dead, it would seem, God changes character. From being a God of mercy who welcomes home the prodigal he becomes an implacable Judge who in the end is prepared to resort to force to secure his aims. His creatures have their chance here on earth; but if they won't take it, then at the end of the line they are for the chop. God would like to win by the methods of love if possible. But if he can't, then he is still going to win.

One can understand why Christians are so frightened of taking a line which would mean disowning much of the Bible as untrue in its simple sense, and having at least to interpret it in a very strained and metaphorical way. For the earliest Church the Old Testament was all the Bible they had. These were the Scriptures in which they found the prophecies of Christ. No wonder they clung to them, even when this created problems. But even orthodox theology does not succeed in saving the Bible for us 100 per cent. All it does is to lose the best bits: 'God so loved the world that he gave...', 'God was in Christ reconciling the world to himself,' and, of course, St. John's epoch-making cry of faith, 'God is love.' You cannot say, 'God IS love' unless he is love essentially and unalterably, unless he cannot and will not use methods other than those of love.

Much of Christian doctrine down the ages has been the result of the attempt to hold these two incompatible pictures of God, both of which we find in the Bible, together. This shows up most clearly of all in Christian teaching about the Cross. From the very earliest days of Christianity Christians were sensitive to the problem: how could the God of the Old Testament, who was above all the God of perfect justice, be reconciled with the new sense of forgiveness and peace with God which Jesus had planted in their hearts? The answer that suggested itself was that Jesus's death had worked the miracle. Perhaps this death was a sacrifice, like the atonement sacrifices offered in the Temple to expiate the sins of the people, but far greater than these, in fact the sacrifice to end all sacrifices. Or perhaps, as the Old Testament said that everyone who was hanged on a tree was accursed, Jesus had undergone the penalty of sin in our place, so that the justice of God was appeased in that way, and he could let us off. Both these ideas are found in the New Testament. But how can the punishment of the innocent possibly satisfy anything that could be called justice? How can the sacrifice of someone else's life possibly expiate my guilt? And how could a God who required either of these things be either rational or good?

These objections have been raised for centuries. But they seem to make absolutely no difference. Many Christians go on clinging to this traditional picture. Why? Just because it is in the Bible? Or perhaps because we need to believe in such a God, because such a God exempts us from taking the Cross seriously. Perhaps the value of it is precisely that it justifies us when we want to give up the way of love and resort to violence or compulsion as the answer to some intolerable situation. If we had to say that even God had no answer but the Cross, that might be too terrifying.

You may feel that what I have been saying is unfair because in Christian belief it is God himself who pays the penalty or makes the sacrifice. But unfortunately that is not what traditional Christian doctrine says.

Greek thought, in which Christianity grew up, believed that God could not suffer; so the idea of the Trinity was used to get round the difficulty. The Father did not suffer at all. The Son became one of us in order to suffer, so that he could make the necessary offering of pain to the Father to atone for our sins and enable the Father to forgive us. This was clever. If you said, What human Father who was halfway decent would behave like that? you were accused of forgetting that God was not Three but One, and of course the Father was involved heart and soul in what the Son was doing. If you then said, Oh well, the Father did suffer on the Cross then, the answer was, Oh no, you are forgetting that God is not merely One but Three Persons. In other words the Trinity was used as a get-out, rather than as a deeper insight into the nature of God as Love. And this was a tragedy, because actually the Trinity which we celebrate today does hold the key to an understanding of God as pure and eternal love without any doubletalk. Let me tell you, in the form of a story which I know is naive, the essence of how and why God deals with us as he does, as I myself see it.

Before any universe existed the life of God was like that of a supremely happy family of the kindest, wisest and most thoroughly good people, only raised to an infinite degree. One day the Father said to the Son, 'We have all this happiness. How sad that there aren't endless others to share it with us. Let's make a universe!' And the Son agreed. And the glory that surrounded them, which was the Holy Spirit of their love for each other, became even brighter, and a voice said, 'Amen!'

Then the Father's face grew sad. 'Ah,' he said, 'but our happiness is our love for each other, which has always been so and never can be otherwise. In a universe our creatures would have to learn love by learning to care for each other of their own free will. That means that they will have to bear with pain and loss; and they will make mistakes; and they won't understand why. And in their fear and perplexity they will make things worse for themselves than they need be; and their vision of us will become dim, and they will say, "It's all nonsense – there is no joy, no meaning in it all." How can we put them to such a risk? And yet it could be so wonderful for them in the end. It seems sad.'

But the Son replied: 'There is a way. I will go and share their lives, including all the pain and loss. Even as one of them my love for you will come through; and they will see that they too can trust you as their Father, and that all their mistakes and pain are only the way to joy.' 'But how can I let you do this?' said the Father. 'How can we be happy,' answered the Son, 'keeping our joy in each other to ourselves, when it could be shared at the cost of just a little suffering, which will be more than worth it if only your plan can be fulfilled. For your sake I want to go.'

And the glory shone even brighter. And the voice of the Holy Spirit said: 'Then I shall go through all the universe and be present to their hearts. And they will realise not just that we love them, but that we love each other; and that even for us love means giving and receiving, caring and being cared for, freely accepting pain to bring joy to those we love, and humbly accepting that sacrifice from those who love us. Then they will understand that that and nothing else is what love is, and that it has been all round them from the very foundation of the world, and that they were made simply to be taken up into the inexhaustible happiness of an eternal family of love. Once they grasp that, then all shall indeed be well.'

'For love is of God; and every one that loveth is born of God and knoweth God . . . God is love; and he that dwelleth in love dwelleth in God, and God in him.'

Preached in the Grosvenor Chapel, London, at the
Silver Jubilee of the William Temple Association,
16 June 1979.

21

The Extremism of Jesus

There was a man of the Pharisees, named Nico-
demus, a ruler of the Jews. The same came to Jesus
by night. John 3. 1

IT IS PERHAPS not entirely fanciful to see you, the members of the
William Temple Association in the figure of Nicodemus. Many of
you are, or are on the way to becoming, people of authority and
responsibility in the life of the nation. Because of your university
or professional training you are in a fundamental sense in the
position of teachers in society. Moreover, the very *raison d'être* of
this Association is to come to Jesus in order to find what he has to
say to the issues of our generation, and what he would have us do
about them. Indeed, with happy memories of this Chapel, of
Liddon House, and of the pub just up the road, one could even say
that quite a lot of this coming to Jesus is, like that of Nicodemus,
done by night.

But my reasons for wanting to share with you some thoughts
about Nicodemus go deeper than these rather artificial and ser-
monistic connections. We are here to give thanks for twenty-five
years of honourable and useful life, during which the William
Temple Association has not only helped its own members to help
each other toward Christian maturity but has also made its con-
tributions to the good of Church and nation. We are celebrating
an achievement, and doing so in the right way by giving thanks
to God 'without whom nothing is strong, nothing is holy.' But if I
read and listen aright, this anniversary also has its notes of hesi-
tancy and self-questioning. Like many other groups in a changing world you are asking, 'What ought we to be doing?', and 'How
ought we to be doing it?' Whenever there are worries about
keeping up numbers, when other people are not instantly enth-
used, the natural reaction is to wonder, 'What is going wrong?'

It is right to face that doubt. If people do not want to join us in any enterprise, or cannot see its value, the reason may well be that the enterprise itself is irrelevant or that we are pursuing it badly. But that is not bound to be the reason. Having a lot of friends, even among the intelligent and high-minded, is no proof either that we are doing the right things or that we are doing them the right way. Vice versa, shrinking numbers do not necessarily mean we are wrong. The followers of Jesus ought to be the last to fall for that one. All that matters is that we should be in the company of those who can properly be called followers of Jesus, because we share something of his way of looking at things and doing them.

But that, of course, is precisely the problem: what does it mean to talk of Jesus's way of looking at things, his way of doing things, when the world we have to look at is so different from his, and the options on what to do are so unimaginably more complex than those that were open to him? So one of the fundamental things we share with Nicodemus is a certain hesitation. 'Rabbi, we know that thou art a teacher come from God, for no man can do these miracles that thou doest except God be with him.' And miracles have been done. The very fact that the world has heard of Jesus at all is perhaps the biggest miracle of the lot – not to mention that nine hundred million people either worship him as God or worship God through him as the supreme teacher and example of what God is like. Then there are all the works of mercy, the triumphs of art, the transformations of human ideals and attitudes. Many would argue that it is the Christian tradition which has provided the vital conditions for the emergence of modern science. That is not a bad list to have sprung from one man's inspiration, even though there are also plenty of tares among the wheat. Certainly no other single figure in history can rival it. So: 'Rabbi, we know that thou art a teacher come from God' – BUT....

Poor Nicodemus never even got as far as the 'but'. The commentators talk carelessly about Jesus answering his question; but, of course, he never actually asks one. Jesus replies to the hesitation, the perplexity behind the words. 'Except a man be born again, he cannot see the Kingdom of God'; it is invisible to him. 'Many', St John tells us in the verses immediately preceding this story, 'believed in his name when they saw the signs which he did, but Jesus did not trust himself to them ... for he himself knew what was in man.' Nicodemus is one of those many. He knows there is visible, tangible, authenticated evidence which forces any intelligent person with decent values to take Jesus seriously. That surely is a good starting-point. But Jesus rebuffs him: 'You don't know what it means to say that something comes "from God", and you never will unless you begin your life over again from scratch.'

This is a pretty brutal challenge. Let us try to understand it in terms of our own situation. Why does Nicodemus take Jesus seriously? Because the things Jesus does seem to Nicodemus the kind of things God would sponsor and approve. But in fact Nicodemus's only reason for thinking that God approves such things is that he, Nicodemus, approves them. 'God' is a label for the highest Nicodemus can envisage, his 'ultimate concern', if you like. Jesus does not trust himself to such people, because he knows that as soon as he does something in obedience to God which they do not approve they will disown him. To see the Kingdom, the absolute sovereignty of God in action, it is necessary to trust Jesus whatever he does – in fact, to trust Jesus, full-stop. But that means being born again, or what the other Evangelists call, 'becoming as a little child'.

The Nicodemus trap is sprung for all of us at one time or another. Very often what we call 'working out the implications of Christianity for today's world' is no more than an exercise in commending Christianity by saying, 'Look! Christianity supports these policies which all right-minded people will obviously approve.' Rabbi, we know that you are a teacher come from God, because (miraculously) your two-thousand-year-old words imply redistribution of wealth, race and sex equality, concern for the environment. And, of course, the swings of circumstance can bring back into fashion some very old-fashioned notions. A modest degree of asceticism, for instance, the simple life, is suddenly seen by 'Rich Christians in an Age of Hunger' to be both morally admirable in a world of shrinking and unevenly shared resources and also just what the doctor ordered for obese and sclerotic Western believers. 'JESUS RIGHT AGAIN', the headlines might cry.

BUT. There is always that 'But' lying in wait for those who start from Nicodemus's end. There are all these good points about

Jesus, *but* there are others we are not so sure about. 'Blessed are you who are poor, who mourn, who hunger' – 'Resist not evil' – 'I saw Satan fall as lightning' – 'This kind comes out only through prayer' – 'Till seventy times seven' – 'Seek ye first the Kingdom of God and his righteousness.' Again we come back to the Kingdom of God. Is that Kingdom a state of affairs to be engineered so prudently that one day there are no more poor, no more evils to resist, no more sins to forgive? (In which case what relevance can it possibly have to those suffering now?) Or is it something here and now, manifested amid and through all the evils by God's holy servant Jesus, something which his Spirit seeks to create in us, something which will eventually be fulfilled in *God's* Brave New World, not ours? The former kind of Kingdom we can all see or foresee in our enthusiastic theorising. The latter is the Kingdom we cannot see, unless we have our eyes opened by Jesus to gaze for the first time in innocence on the world as it really is.

No Christian in his generation did more than William Temple to encourage solid and constructive efforts to deal with the problems of injured and oppressed humanity. But in a famous passage in his *Readings in St John's Gospel* he also wrote: 'We cannot call upon the Creator Spirit, by whose aid The World's foundations first were laid, in order to use omnipotence for the supply of our futile pleasures or the success of our futile plans.' There is no proper human life without society, without government, without plans of some sort. They ought to be as good as we can make them. But that is only half the story of human need, and the less radical half. When we look at history (and there is no need to look further than our own century) we can see clearly that the truly intractable problem is not that of the things we do but what makes us do them, not our follies and crimes but the seemingly inexhaustible capacity for evil which produces them and distorts and frustrates every plan of our devising. Only God can master that dragon; and his Kingdom is seen in all its distinctive power and character not where the cancerous results of evil are cut out but where the underlying malfunction is put right.

But spiritual cleansing from evil is brought about not by the balanced sensible morality of decent people, precious though that is, but by the crazy extremism of Jesus and those who truly follow him – by poverty and sacrifice, by prayer and fasting, pursued not for their own sakes but as means to the healing, transfiguring, liberating power of divine love which is as different from human benevolence in its effectiveness as the sun from a sunray lamp. If you want new life to flow through your Association as you enter your second quarter-century, you must give yourselves not only to an intelligent understanding and communication of the faith, not only to coping with the needs of the world, but also to an individual and corporate spiritual life which does not evaluate Jesus but trusts and follows him.

22 The Meaning of Repentance

THERE IS NOT one of us here, I am sure, who has not been helped in some way by the life of this church: by the evening Low Mass, ordering our days in God's peace; by the 'Take up thy bed and walk' of the confessional; by the exhilaration of the yearly round of festivals, printing the pattern of redemption on the deepest, barely conscious levels of our hearts.

But not all of us, perhaps, have found so much help in St. Mary Magdalene herself; and one possible reason for this may be the rather unbalanced emotional response to her in Christian tradition. Christians have seemed uneasy in their handling of her, swinging between the sentimental and the morbid. You can see this in art. On the one side there is the large number of paintings which portray nothing more than a voluptuous lady with a rather off-putting expression. But there is another, darker side, of which the supreme example is Donatello's statue, surely one of the most terrifying great works in European art.

Donatello chose to present the Magdalene in extreme old age, not merely with no vestige left of her one-time beauty, but utterly ravaged. Her body, skeletal with fasting, is clothed in rags; her eyes, blank with weeping, stare out above cheeks as hollow as those of a dead woman; the mouth is half-open in wordless pain, the hands held up, fingertips apart in timid supplication. The statue is a work of genius, of that there can be no doubt whatever. But it is also a total denial of everything the Gospel stands for. This Magdalene is still in agony, still crushed by the burden of the past, still beseeching mercy. This is never the woman who, as the Gospel tells us, was freed from seven devils by the Lord, or who heard him say, 'Her sins which are many are forgiven, for she loved much.'

The problem of which these works of art are symptomatic is a fundamental one for Christians, and we can perhaps get a clue to it by considering another oddity about the Magdalene in Christian devotion. In order to become an authorised Christian saint you have, as you know, to be classified. It is no good just being yourself. You cannot enter the calendar simply as a name, as, let us say, plain Dorothy Shrimpton or Charles Smith. You must also have a label: Apostle, Martyr, Bishop, Confessor, and so forth. Now one feels that there may have been certain perplexities in deciding into which of the conventional categories to put St. Mary Magdalene. Be that as it may, in the end the matter was resolved by giving her a pigeonhole all to herself, that of 'Penitent'.

The words 'penitent' and 'penitence' play a large part in Christian piety. But significantly they play no part at all in the New Testament. What the New Testament is talking about constantly is 'repentance', which is a very different matter. Penitence is sorrow for sin. Sometimes it is no more than an immature sorrow which is distressed only because we have spoiled our good opinion of ourselves. But it can be a more adult sorrow which grieves over the harm we have done to others and the wounds we have inflicted on the loving hearts of those who care for us, not only men and women but God. As such, penitence is right and necessary – let there be no mistake about that. We ought always to be sorry for our sins, and more sorry indeed than most of us usually are. But even at its best penitence is only a first step; and it is absolutely essential that we go beyond it.

The danger of penitence is that unless we do go further it inevitably turns into one of two things: egotism or despair. The idea of the penitent as egotistical may seem surprising at first, but it is not really so. Egotists are not necessarily self-satisfied but they are self-absorbed. They are more interested in themselves, even in their own failings, than in anyone or anything else. We all know the sort of person who can go on for hours developing the theme, 'Of course the trouble with *me* is . . .' In the confessional such people proceed to do the priest's job for him; so much so that when at last they ask for 'counsel, penance and absolution' one is tempted to ask, 'Are you sure you want counsel? Wouldn't a tape-recorder do?' Such people soon cease to be truly sorry about their sins. They are merely fascinated by them.

At the other extreme are those tragic souls who are enslaved by sorrow. For them the words of the Psalmist have come true in a way the poet never intended: 'My sins have taken such hold upon me that I am not able to look up; yea, they are more in number than the hairs of my head, and my heart hath failed me.' They are hooked on guilt and remorse. In some the trouble is that they lack all belief in themselves; their sorrow for sin is an attempt to win desperately needed reassurance from God or Man. In others, the trouble is an equally implacable pride. They can never come to terms with their own failure, or consent to receive reinstatement as a gift from another person, not even from God. So penitence turns to despair, because they are trapped in it. They cannot take that vital second step beyond.

What is that second step? It is the step from penitence to repentance. And what is the difference? It has been splendidly summed up in the words of a great New Testament scholar: '*Repentance is joy that God is so gracious.*' Repentance is realising the simple fact that the worse our sins have been, the more amazing is the grace that pardons them and loves them into hope and newness of life. In other words, we ought always to be more delighted at the goodness of those who forgive us than we are distressed at the wrongdoing they have had to forgive. The fact that the Magdalene had got it right was made plain by the dramatic outpouring of her love for Jesus, when she washed his feet with her tears and wiped them with the hairs of her head and anointed them. The words of Jesus on that occasion precisely underline this element of joyful love in true repentance: 'Her sins, which are many, have indeed been forgiven; you can tell that because she loves so much.'

You may think it far-fetched to pick on this as the heart of the matter of repentance. But it is not, because this and nothing else is the first, essential result of that total transformation of outlook and attitude to life which is the meaning of the New Testament word we translate 'repentance'. Of this transformation Mary Magdalene is a magnificent example; and therein lies one secret of her sainthood – as it is of all sainthood. What is this secret? I am not sure that I can explain it very well, because I am still struggling to get it clear in my own mind; but let my try it very briefly this way. Some of you may have read the spiritual diary of the late Pope John, *Journal of a Soul*. I wonder if it left you with the same bafflement as it did me? I thought I had never read a book so painfully frank which nevertheless seemed to throw no light at all on what, by the testimony of thousands, the man so manifestly was. There seemed to be an extraordinary abyss between the outer man, so lovable and selfless and sensitive and humorous in all his relations, and the inner man, pernickety and humourless and painfully self-absorbed. The only answer, so far as I could see, was that in the *Journal* one was hearing not the voice of Pope John but the cliches of that obsessive concern with one's own perfection which had been ground into him as a young seminarist. As a friend remarked to me: 'You can't imagine how such an appalling system ever produced such a wonderful man.'

The answer is, of course, that it did not. It is significant that, as the years went by, he plainly found it harder and harder to keep up the *Journal*. He had outgrown its initial assumptions. What produced the saintly Pope was precisely not his concern with himself but his passion for Jesus and for other people, opening him to the transforming grace of God. It is when we lose ourselves in admiration for goodness and generosity nobler than our own, when we allow our actions to be dictated not by some theory of self-improvement but by the deepest needs of other people, that we grow without realising it. And the first, possibly the most crucial step is to accept whatever value we may have as a gift from the love of others, and not to try to create it by our own achievement.

This, all this, Mary Magdalene did. She refused to be imprisoned by the failures of the past; it was enough for her that Jesus believed in her. That step once taken, what changed her was her love and admiration for Jesus and her perception of his needs and those of his friends. Drawn by these things she left her home to care for them in their task of preaching the Gospel; she watched his execution; she came one morning early, while it was yet dark to the dangerous destination of his grave. And there the glory of his resurrection was revealed to her as she wept, wept not because *she* was desolate but because she could not find the body of her friend to show it some last kindness. Those of us who hope to join her in beholding that glory will be well advised to seek it by the same road of happy self-forgetting.

23 An Eye for the Unseen

'HERE BE DRAGONS' ... and the words which the old map-makers used to fill in those large blank areas about which they knew rather less than their customers had a right to expect seem also to have been favourites with those who wrote the lives of the saints. Indeed, the parallel is closer still. For, just as the map-makers would cheerfully conjecture whole continents where none in fact existed, as in the North Pacific, so the hagiographers felt it their duty to make up the deficiencies of church history with a plentiful supply of the kind of saints a really interesting Church *ought* to have had. Of these our patron, Saint Margaret of Antioch, is an example.

The story goes that Margaret was the Christian daughter of a pagan priest in Pisidian Antioch, the modern Konya in south central Turkey. She rejected the advances of the local Imperial governor, and was denounced by him as a Christian. The tortures to which she was subjected included being swallowed by a dragon (Satan in disguise) which then burst and she stepped out unharmed. (Satan, as a fallen angel and so a spiritual being, was not unfortunately finished off by this experience, and lived to fight another day.) Finally, Margaret was beheaded. She is shown in art with a dragon, usually writhing under her feet.

In Christian piety, especially in the Western church, St Margaret is often shown with St Katherine of Alexandria, a lady equally unfortunate in her experiences but a great deal more dangerous. She was not only beautiful and good, but nobly born and extremely learned. (Those familiar with the vanity and cowardice of the male sex will not be surprised to learn that she was unmarried.) She took upon herself to convince the Emperor of the folly of idol-worship. He marshalled fifty learned philosophers against her; and when these luckless academics failed to defeat her in argument, they were burned alive. The Emperor then showed that he had not become Emperor for nothing by offering to marry her; but she turned him down, and in his rage he had her flogged and imprisoned. Next an attempt was made to kill her by breaking her on a spiked wheel, but it shattered; and though she was unhurt several unfortunate bystanders were killed by flying fragments. Two hundred soldiers lining the square then announced, with more enthusiasm than sense, their own conversion to Christianity; and were instantly beheaded for their pains. On the principle that the simplest methods are the best, Katherine too was then beheaded, and the angels carried her body off to Mount Sinai.

So, you see, when we move from St Margaret's Church this evening to St Katherine's Chapel Garden for our evening party, and you look up at the statue of St Katherine in its niche, and note the spiked wheel, there is a connection between the two saints. There was a time in the history of Christian Europe when these two figures were the prime symbols and representatives of a complex ideal of popular religion, and were naturally associated as such. This church and that garden call to mind a whole world of faith.

It is, of course, a world that for us has totally passed away. First, our ideal of a saint is quite different. People are sometimes quite disappointed to learn that this church is not dedicated to St Margaret of Scotland, a kind, intelligent, practical woman, who as Queen bore her husband, King Malcolm Canmore, five children, and exercised an immense influence for good over his policies. Today, a saint must be one of us, involved in ordinary people's lives, helping, healing, comforting. They may be far beyond us in prayer and self-sacrifice and holiness, but basically we rate them on the same standards of human achievement by which we judge everyone. Magic and miracle mean little to us. Even a martyrdom is to some extent spoiled for us by all these supernatural stage-effects. And secondly, our universe is so different from the one in terms of which these stories were written. God, for us, no longer behaves like the Wizard of Oz; and if we thought he did we would no longer respect him.

But one of the great things we can learn from being a Christian is not to be trapped narrowly in the culture and ideas of our own century. We are fellow-citizens of the Kingdom of God with all these other people who went before us, who followed Jesus as Lord with perhaps deeper devotion than we, who often lived lives of heroic goodness which put ours to shame. Can we just dismiss their piety with words like 'preposterous', as the reference books tend to do nowadays? They may have been credulous about fantastic stories, about the possibilities of the world. They may have made up these tales because they found them in some way edifying or comforting. But when we look at the Church today, can we afford just to be superior? Might it not be better to ask what they were trying to say, what this vanished world of faith might have to teach us that we have lost?

Underneath the stories of St Margaret and St Katherine we can still detect a real historical situation, that of the increasingly savage persecutions that kept breaking out against Christianity in the third and four centuries of our era, until the Roman Empire became Christian under Constantine in the year 314. If we look at the more sober historians of the period we see the factual ingredients that the writers of saintly romances used and elaborated. The raping of Christian women during and after arrest; the offers of release in exchange for their favours. The use of torture and inhuman punishments to make Christians recant. Such things are the routine of tyranny, and our century has seen more of them than most, not seldom still directed against Christians and other religious believers. Nor need we doubt that the steadfastness of those who refused to give in did many times convert the basically decent and distressed onlooker. After all, that too still happens today. And another thing. If you read the ancient historians who first recorded the history of those times, you find that there are very few sensational and miraculous tales. There was no expectations that this sort of thing, exploding wheels, expiring dragons, and so forth, would happen for ordinary people. Nor were the general run of Christians demoralised when it did not. They still went bravely and cheerfully to their deaths.

The stories are not about what might happen to you if only you were good enough or believed strongly enough; and there is no evidence that the readers who provided such an insatiable market for them ever thought they were. That is not what a miracle story, whether in the Bible or in Christian tradition, is really about. A miracle story is telling us something, trying to pass on a particular message: that behind appearances there is another, greater reality. The story of St Margaret was saying that behind the torture and murder of *every* defenceless Christian girl the eternal reality was that evil had been humiliated and overthrown. The story of St Katherine was saying that *every* time a Christian went with unwavering faith to his or her death, the specious arguments of worldly philosophy were discredited and shown to be false, and the truth of things was proclaimed in a way that would convince and convert ordinary people more mightily than any other. The exuberant fantasy of the legends is simply a way of making concrete the hidden facts of the spiritual order, of showing the reader what was really going on, so that we should not be taken in by the appearance of seeming defeat. In this the stories simply follow the pattern set by the Gospel itself, where the stark horror of the death of Christ is shown to be the eternal triumph of goodness and love. They dramatise the faith of the Creeds, which tell us that for those with eyes to see even the whole mystery of Godhead could be set forth in the life of one human being.

Once we grasp this, we can see that to describe such stories as preposterous merely shows how arrogantly limited and superficial our view of life has become. Our preference for saints who do practical good is not really based on faith but on lack of it: a measure of visible achievement is real enough for us to take an interest in. We have lost our eye for the spiritual realities where, as in the Cross of Christ, solid victory appears outwardly as defeat. And this loss of the vision of faith has its effects in other ways: in a tendency to compromise, to dismiss as stupid the life of poverty, love, non-violence, equal openness to all, to which Christ calls us. When we read of St Margaret rejecting the immoral proposals of the provincial governor, perhaps we regard it in a modern superficial way as no more than exaggerated loyalty to the sexual conventions of a particular age, ones not sympathetic today; whereas in fact it stood for something far more profound, a fierce commitment with the whole of oneself to a personal integrity, a desire to express loyalty to goodness and truth with every aspect of one's life and being, whatever the cost. Integrity, wholeness, commitment: these above all are the things most of us lack. We can be glad that our church is dedicated to St Margaret of Antioch, for she symbolises what our too often self-indulgent, superficial discipleship most needs – readiness to suffer for the victory of the things which are not seen, which are eternal.

24 The Integrated Christian

The dove descending breaks the air
With flame of incandescent terror
Of which the tongues declare
The one discharge from sin and error.
The only hope, or else despair
Lies in the choice of pyre or pyre –
To be redeemed from fire by fire.

Who then devised the torment? Love.
Love is the unfamiliar Name
Behind the hands that wove
The intolerable shirt of flame
Which human power cannot remove.
We only live, only suspire
Consumed by either fire or fire.
T.S. Eliot, Little Gidding, ll. 200–213

'THE ONE DISCHARGE from sin and error.' That is a bold claim. The world has been trying to disentangle itself from the effects of its own wickedness and confusion, or at the very least to reduce their frequency, for a very long time now without notable success. More to the point, perhaps, the Christian Churches, who claim to be the ones on whom the Dove did descend in tongues of fire, have also had very patchy and unequal results in their efforts to the same end. Was it all illusion – a light that seemed to presage the dawn but turned out no more than just another guttering candle?

Our notions of what freedom from sin and error would be are in any case pretty limited. Sin, to us, is basically failure to live by the light we have been given. This is mostly a mixture of what our family and our society expect of us, modified by the ideas of the smaller groups in which we live most of our lives. If you are an ex-

ecutive in a big industrial or commercial organisation, your
vision of what you ought to do will be different from that of your
son or daughter at university, both in personal relationships, in
politics and in the question of the work to which to devote one's
life, and how to carry it out. If you live in a village or market town,
your thoughts may well not be those of your offspring who have
taken time out to visit India, not as privileged European tourists
but in far rougher conditions than you or I would readily contem-
plate. In the case of Christians the social formula is somewhat
sharpened up and thrown out of balance by the Ten Commandments and by odd remarks of Jesus which have filtered to us
through sermons and Lent books or some form of Bible study.
This unstable mixture is our Judge, determining our sense of
what is sin and what is not. That sense will be very incomplete
and inadequate, condemning some things in which there is little
or nothing wrong, and taking for granted others that are very
wrong indeed; but we can deepen and enlarge it as life goes on,
provided we are open to God and other people. We must not stop
growing morally once we reach adulthood.

But, granted that we go on seeking more light as years go by,
how do we live by what light we get? The answer most people
would give is that, having taken aboard that love, fair-
mindedness, forgiveness, let us say, are the principles that ought
to control us, we try to make ourselves more loving, fair-minded
and forgiving people. The trouble with this is that in doing so we
inevitably divide ourselves. We split ourselves into the controlling, spiritual part, which knows what ought to be done, and the
recalcitrant emotional or physical part which refuses to be con-
trolled.

But is this ever going to work? It is true that a great deal can be
done by training and habit. If we are the sort of people who are
blessed with a good deal of morale and will-power we can discipline ourselves to be punctilious in fulfilling our obligations, to
be abstemious in food or drink, to keep fit, to get up early, to say
our prayers – which is all very good news for our fellow-citizens.
It is probably also good news for our own bodies – but is it good
news for our souls? Does it make us *integrated* people? – that is,
are our emotions in sympathy with our minds? Or are they
simply being kept under by our desire to be good?

If part of me wants very much to be the sort of person of whom my parents or a particularly important figure in my childhood, like an admired or feared school-teacher, would approve, then part of my emotional vitality will put all its force behind that. But another part may have quite different ideas, and will be perpetually repressed or alienated, made to feel that it doesn't belong to me at all and isn't wanted. In the kingdom of my personality law and order may prevail, but it will be a law and order enforced by a strong and well-paid police force, not one created by the agreed desires of all the citizens.

Christians have very often settled for this kind of goodness. They have tried to impose on their bodies and emotions the kind of rules that they felt described the sort of life Jesus wanted from us. But they have not carried their bodies and feelings with them. It has been a way of life imposed by the mind and will; and this method has been justified by thinking of the mind and will, the spiritual element, as the only part of us that would enjoy eternal life.

But Jesus warned us against precisely this mistake. 'A house divided against itself falleth', he said. If we would have a happy, spontaneous Christian life, one that does the loving, honest, courageous thing of itself, then we need above all else that all the parts of our personality be lined up in the same direction, not fighting each other but moving supportively together. And this will be achieved not by turning in on ourselves, by one part, the reflective, thinking part, trying to put the rest in order, but by something from outside ourselves drawing us, every part of us, in the same direction. It is as we respond with the whole of ourself, mind and heart and body, to some call from *outside* ourselves, that we really become integrated, unified. This call may, alas, be an evil call. The false god of the totalitarian state, whether it be the Fascist or the Communist, is an instance. It can give the individual peace within the self, unifying every talent, affection and energy, in the service of an iniquitous idea. But that only exemplifies the general rule that 'the worst kind of corruption is the corruption of what is best.' For the true unifying force, the one that delivers us from the inner bondage of lust, indolence and prejudice, 'the one discharge from sin and error', is also one that comes from outside – and that is our neighbour's need.

'Love – Love is the unfamiliar name.' Love, you may say, is not a particularly unfamiliar name today. We hear it all too often, from pop singers and from pulpits. But love in Christ's sense of the word *is* unfamiliar. It is a selfless response to the need of our neighbour, whoever that neighbour may be. And to their true need, not just what we think is good for them or what they deserve. And without limit or qualification, not just as much as we think we think we can manage. All this means a freedom from prejudice, from convention, a freedom of imagination and sensitivity, which can be hard to bear – an 'intolerable shirt of flame', far more painful than the hair shirt of the ascetic concerned only with self-improvement. But this and this alone will work the miracle. It is as we see, and rouse ourselves to answer, the silent plea in the eyes of the suffering person next door, or at work, or in the street; the cowed and friendless child at our child's school; the silent man or woman who sits behind a pillar at church; that our powers are distracted from the civil war of 'being good', and are liberated to work together in self-forgetting love, and to involve our families, neighbours, friends and fellow-Christians in the same.

And what is true of the individual is true also of the community, of the Church itself. For we may take it as a law of the Spirit that in so far as the Church thinks in terms of rules and ideals of holiness, and how these things can be fostered within the structures of eccleciastical life by prayer and study, it will undoubtedly fail. But in so far as it looks outwards – to ask what response the Church ought to be making to the needs of humankind, how it can forward God's purpose of drawing all his children into one family, how it can meet the legitimate doubts and perplexities of men and women in a scientific age honestly and with understanding, how it can change the hearts and policies of the world so that the rich do not go on getting richer, and the poor poorer, the strong stronger and the weak weaker – in short, if it seeks first the Kingdom of God and his righteousness, not the Kingdom of the Church and the righteousness of Christians, then all else will be added unto it. Is it not true, for example, that that unity which seems so impossible when we look inwards, seems indispensable as we look outwards at the work waiting to be done?

'The only hope, or else despair, lies in the choice of pyre or pyre.' The demand upon us is simply this: 'How can we help to make the life of the human family where we are more like the life of the family of God?" It is as we face that demand and try to meet it, day by day, in things small as well as great, that we are redeemed from the fire of sin and error, feeding upon our souls, by the flame of love, offering itself upon the altar of another's need. One destroys. The other springs up, pure and unquenchable, to eternal life.

25 True Humility

HUMILITY IS A tricky subject to talk about. For one thing it is a very rare virtue, so the chances are that anyone who does talk about it hasn't got it, and is therefore not really qualified to do so. On the other hand those who are genuinely humble don't think they are, and would never dream of talking as if they were experts in the matter. As for those who actually claim humility, well, it's the first and most elementary rule of the game that they are disqualified from the start, like the man who said, 'My fault – if I have a fault – is excessive modesty.'

This being so it is a trifle disconcerting to hear St Paul, in the Acts of the Apostles, telling the Ephesian elders: 'Ye know . . . after what manner I have been with you at all seasons, serving the Lord with all humility of mind.' That is not how a real saint should be talking. It is a great comfort, then, to find that in his letters in the New Testament Paul never claims the virtue of humility for himself, though he does commend it as something that ought to be a mark of Christians in general. What has almost certainly happened in the Book of Acts is that the author has followed the general practice of ancient historians, and put into the mouth of his hero what *he* thought would be an edifying speech for this particular occasion. No doubt he worked into it various people's recollections of the scene; but basically it is his idea of what Paul's spiritual testament ought to have said, and as a devoted friend and admirer of Paul he wanted to make it clear that Paul practised what he preached. He was an example, not a 'Do-as-I-say-not-as-I-do' man.

So Paul passes the first elementary test, and so, of course, do all really good people. And if they urge us to be humble, as they do, they never claim to be shining examples themselves – in fact, much more important than that, they really don't think they are humble. But they are quite clear that humility is one of the most vital Christian virtues, and that an un-humble Christian is a contradiction in terms. Why is this?

First and very much foremost, because of the humility of God. God, who knows everything, has everything, can do everything, became one of us. We say this so often. But do we think at all realistically what it means? It was said of Dean Swift that he is the only writer who ever faced honestly and mentioned in his narratives the ordinary physical facts of being a human animal, because, for example, when describing Gulliver in Lilliput he took into account what would actually be involved in a man's need to relieve himself at regular intervals. Most writers, even the so-called realistic ones, mention such things only to shock; Swift, and perhaps James Joyce, did it to try to open our eyes to what we actually are. To do this is very difficult, for most of us have a highly censored picture of ourselves and of human kind in general. And so when we think of God becoming Man, we think of him becoming someone with a brilliant mind, a loving heart, great courage and compassion, a compelling personality, penetrating eyes, a moving voice, and so on. We do not think that it meant becoming a helpless baby who had to be fed and changed and cleaned up, that it meant having a runny nose and being sick and having your stomach turned by the sores of beggars lying in the street, and in the end enduring the humiliating physical effects of scourging (as described, for example, by Lawrence of Arabia in *The Seven Pillars of Wisdom*) as well as the more dramatically acceptable agonies of crucifixion. And into all this he came from heaven, from pure spiritual blessedness, from the adoration of beings as far superior to us as we are to the plankton in the sea.

No wonder then that for many Christians, from St Paul onwards, the first lesson of the Incarnation has been that we should never think ourselves too good for anything life may bring. It is this which down the centuries has taken tens of thousands of comfortable upper and middle class Christians to tend with their own hands the leprous, the crippled, the outcast and the mentally ill of every nation. 'Have this mind in you which was also in Christ Jesus, who being in the form of God thought it not a prize to be on an equality with God, but emptied himself, taking the form of a servant . . .'

This is the first, great mark of humility, that we think nothing beneath us, nothing and no one. No task too undignified, no person unworthy of our service. St Vincent de Paul, the seven-

teenth century Frenchman who was one of the greatest organis-
ers of practical charity who ever lived, and who found in a Europe
ravaged by the Wars of Religion more than enough scope for his
talents, recruited many hundreds of men and women to his work.
Some were aristocrats, some simple but respectable country
girls, the first Sisters of Charity. In letters and talks he gave
them an immense wealth of spiritual and practical advice, but
one phrase came again and again. He spoke always of 'our
masters, the poor', 'the poor, our masters'. And he showed this
spirit in a hundred ways himself, but I mention one. Even in late
life, when he was the busiest as well as the most revered man in
France, he would himself attend to the needs of some idiot boys
who had been found in the grounds of his headquarters at St
Lazare when his order took it over. Nothing, nobody is beneath
us.

This is still a practical inspiration to us today. You do not have
to be a Mother Teresa in Calcutta. Here at home there are a thousand obscure but vital ways to serve those who, compared with
ourselves, are 'the poor' – if not in money then in some very important aspect of human life. Helping people is the most 'labour-
intensive' industry of all. A youngster who is in trouble with the
police; a home where the mother just can't cope; a family with an
elderly relative who is wandery or incontinent; someone who has
had treatment in a mental hospital but still needs constant
support; autistic or sub-normal children; the range is almost
endless, the work often wearying beyond belief or menial or
sordid. Official welfare workers, however excellent, are grossly
over-burdened, and there are many things that can be done by
untrained or lightly trained people. Is this not a vocation to
which Christians especially ought to respond? But certainly
such service calls for humility.

But is there not a danger, you may ask, that those who serve
others in this way may think of themselves as practising humility, and so cease to be humble? Of course, this is perfectly true.
And the question takes us to the heart of what humility means.
Humility is nothing to do with false modesty, pretending to be
other than we are. When we say that nothing and no one is
beneath us, we do not mean that we are claiming to be stupider,
lazier or wickeder than anyone else. It simply means that just as
Christ, who was the Eternal Son of God, thought no human task

or condition beneath him, so we, however wise or good we may be, are prepared to undertake any task or any deprivation, in order to help or make contact with another human being, even the most limited or unlovable. But how is it that when we are doing this, we do not think how humble we are being? Because we are not thinking about ourselves at all. We are thinking about the other person. In this again we take our cue from Christ. We see God's command for us in our neighbour's need, just as he saw his Father's will for him in the sick and the sinful whom he met, and the opportunity they presented.

It is worth remembering that if we try to be better Christians by saying to ourselves each day, 'I must be more truthful', or, 'more charitable', or, 'more disciplined', we shall only succeed in making ourselves more egotistical, and humility will never be ours. But if we look outwards at the needs around us, and try to be sensitive to some of the cries for help, spoken or unspoken, that too often go unheeded, truth, charity, self-discipline and all the rest will come without our noticing. In spiritual things too it is true that muscles are best built by doing a job of work, not by exercises in front of a mirror.

Let me end with a story, a true story told me by a friend. Many years ago now this friend was Vicar of a London parish within the area of the Bishop of Kensington, at the time when that Bishop was Henry Montgomery-Campbell. In the parish was an old woman, living alone in one room, who had once been 'on the game'. But now she had made her peace with God, was being prepared for Confirmation, and was looking forward with passionate longing to her first Communion. Suddenly she was taken ill, and soon it became apparent she was dying. My friend assured her it was perfectly proper for her to receive Communion, and urged her to do so, but she refused. Unless she was confirmed it wouldn't feel right. At his wits' end the vicar phoned Bishop Montgomery-Campbell, at about 10 o'clock at night. All the Bishop said was, 'Meet me at the Tube station in one hour.' At 11 my friend was at the local Underground and there came the Bishop's tall figure, striding along with the big case in which he carried his robes. Together they went to the house where the old woman lay dying. In her small room the Bishop robed in full vestments, as he would have done in her parish church, cope, mitre and all; and with the Vicar as his Chaplain confirmed her there in bed. When the Confirmation was over my friend thanked the Bishop and said, 'I can carry on now.' 'Nonsense' came the reply; and the Bishop set up a little altar, and celebrated, and gave her the Sacrament, just as she had so dearly hoped he would do in church. And after that he disrobed, and the two of them stayed in that little room till dawn, when the old woman died in the Bishop's arms. After the necessary arrangements had been made, they went down into the street. 'You will come back to breakfast?' said my friend. 'Sorry', said the Bishop, 'I can't. I promised to say the 8 o'clock this morning for the Vicar of X who is ill.' And off he went, striding back to the Tube. If we let God speak to us through the needs of others, and think only of them, humility will come, precisely because we shall never know that it has done so.

26 Prayer and Fasting

Preached in St Margaret's, Westminster,
29 July 1979.

THE HEALING OF the epileptic boy was a task which proved too much for Jesus's disciples. But clearly they expected to be able to do it: for afterwards they asked him privately, 'Why could not we cast the demon out?' Jesus's words to the boy's father have already indicated one reason: lack of faith. 'All things are possible to him who believes.' Now, in reply to the disciples, he mentions another: lack of prayer. 'This kind cannot be driven out by anything but prayer.'

Prayer and faith: faith and prayer. Two sides of the same coin. Two things which depend on one another. Without faith prayer becomes a leaden and lifeless burden. 'He who comes to God must believe that he exists,' says the Epistle to the Hebrews, 'and that he is one who rewards those who diligently seek him.' If God is unreal, just an attractive but dubious theory, how can we pray? how can we feel it, deep inside, to be anything but a waste of time? But equally, the less we pray, the less real God becomes. If we never take time to be with God, to pay attention to him alone, to see life in the new light that falls upon it when he is accepted as the biggest fact of all, the vision fades, the heart grows cold, and faith sinks down to dead ashes.

Over and over again people say: 'How can I believe? How can I have more faith?' – just like the father in the story. But what is one to say to them? Pray? Keep on praying and faith will come? But without faith how can they pray? Prayer is the characteristic activity of those who believe. Faith is the characteristic virtue of those who pray. It is a whole different scene, a world on its own. The question is: how do you get into it?

There are many ways in. But most of them are not ones that can be handed out from a pulpit. We do not find them by responding to argument, or by being moved by fine words. One of the most frequent is that we meet someone whose life has a completely different quality. It is not so much that they are more patient, more

112

kind, more happy, more generous – though they may well be all these things. It is that they see things, judge things, react to things quite differently. We get a disconcerting sense that their values, their responses to people and situations are much more like those God would have. We feel very limited, very petty and immature. Not that they condemn us, but they speak their mind. It is not a pious act they are putting on. It is their natural self.

And we discover – for they never tell you – that prayer is the one thing they cannot do without, the area of life they guard most jealously. The world such people live in is clear, solid, sharp; they are open to reality – people, things – and to the joys and sorrows of existence with a directness of feeling, but at the same time a courage and stability that make one long to be like them. They show us that there is so much more to human life than we had realised. Theoretical arguments about prayer and faith, for or against, seem neither here nor there. We simply know there is something there to be found which we cannot pass up, and unless we do something about it we shall be restless and dissatisfied all our days.

A book, a poem, a work of art, a piece of music may have a similar effect. We become aware of a door opening, a gate into a wider world, or perhaps just a line to be stepped across, like the brooks in *Through the Looking Glass*. Of course, once we step across there is still a long journey, and a hard one, and we may not persevere. But a way has been opened to us, a way to a new kind of experience of the world, in which God becomes, or begins to become, real, and so all other beings are known for the first time as his creatures, his children, his family, and the life that flows through them as his love.

So, in our story, prayer and faith are the ways of living which open this particular situation, the one at the centre of which the epileptic boy has put a destructive question-mark, to the reality of God and the life that flows from his love. To take a scientific parable, the rigid tragic evil is placed within a new and larger field of force, and everything begins to rearrange itself into a new pattern. The force is not in those who pray and believe; they do not practise these things in order to become men and women of power or healing. It is in God who gets access to the tragedy, can bring his re-creating love to bear on the problem, *because they are in the situation to let him into it.*

But is there no special life-style, no training or discipline that can help us to be the kind of men and women who let God into the tangles and deadlocks of the world? As a matter of fact there is, and it was pin-pointed by the very last word of Jesus' reply: 'This kind cometh not out but by prayer and fasting'. There is in fact doubt whether Jesus mentioned 'fasting' or just 'prayer' in answer to the disciples' question, for many ancient manuscripts leave the word out, and most modern translations follow these rather than the ones that include it. But fasting, then as now, was a mark of especially holy or spiritual people; Jesus himself fasted in the wilderness; and we would be very arrogant to dismiss it as a worthless or outmoded idea.

What do we mean by 'fasting?' In one sense lots of people fast: they do it to try and get a slim and attractive figure, to protect health, and to prolong life. There is a general relevance to prayer here, simply because it is as hard to pray as to do anything else if you are sluggish from too much food or drink.

What about Christian fasting? It used to be a widespread custom to receive Holy Communion fasting, but only a minority do so now. Even in the Roman Church the rules have been so relaxed that fasting in the old sense has almost gone. During Lent it is nowadays thought rather pointless to fast unless you give the money you save to a good cause. The odd thing is this: both these practices of fasting were to help people to pray, but this has been completely forgotten.

Fasting is, of course, only one aspect of the general discipline of the body. If we are even to have time to pray, to say nothing of praying well, we have to give up something: a part of the time we would have spent on TV or reading or sleep or social life, and so forth. But while people may recognise that self-denial in these ways may be unavoidable, they rather gird at the idea of fasting – going without food and drink. Perhaps this is a symptom of the fact that our society is grossly over-fed. We have come to accept this level of overfeeding as essential to our health, and regard going without as cranky and dangerous.

We may begin to see some spiritual point in fasting, if we approach it from another angle. At this moment a thousand million people are getting less food than the minimum needed to maintain health, and four hundred million are slowly dying of diseases caused by malnutrition. And that in a world where there is in fact enough food produced now for all to have all they need if it were fairly shared. Not all these people are in the Third World; some are here in Britain, old people living alone, for instance.

Do we care? Of course we do. We pray, we protest, we give to Christian Aid. But is it *real* to us? It cannot be real to us so long as we do not open ourselves to that experience, so long as we are anaesthetised by our full stomachs. Just once in my life, and that not for long, I had to go without food because I had no money. It was a piffling minor hardship not worth talking about; but it gave me a glimpse I have never forgotten of what it might be like to be in that position again and again with no prospect of rescue such as I had. No doubt some of you have known the grim reality at much closer quarters. But if we are lucky and have enough, it matters desperately that, if age and strength permit, we should open ourselves regularly to a taste of the hard realities with which our fellow human beings have to live. Not just to stir our imaginations, though that is important, but to show God we mean it when we pray, at least to carry their cross a step or two even if we are not to be crucified on it.

That then is one simple and very elementary first level in which fasting is related to prayer, especially intercession. Because fasting is such a basic form of self-denial, a threatening gesture against our instinct of self-preservation, it can serve as a means of inner identification not just with the hungry but with all the deprived.

But there is a deeper level. To satisfy hunger is one of the strongest of all urges, stronger than fatigue, sex, aggression. Deliberately to go hungry, therefore, is to put the very highest rating on what you are doing instead. When that is prayer, you are saying to God, 'I want to show you how much you mean to me.' Fasting, if done for the right motive, makes prayer an expression of love, a costly attempt to open oneself to the greatest of all realities, God. To that sincerity, God responds; and those who make that sacrifice learn that God *is* real, and become channels of his life-giving love in the world.

In conclusion, two practical points. First, how you should fast and how much, is a matter for experienced advice in the light of your health and particular circumstances. Consult someone, priest, religious or lay person, who is wise in the spiritual life, and if need be, your doctor. Secondly, remember our Lord's words: 'When you fast, anoint your head and wash your face that your fasting may not be seen by men but by your Father who is in secret; and your Father who sees in secret will reward you.'

27 Lies

*'And Jezebel wrote in the letters, "Proclaim a fast,
and set Naboth on high among the people; and set
two base fellows opposite him, and let them bring a
charge against him, saying, 'You have cursed God
and the king.' Then take him out, and stone him to
death."' I Kings 21.9–10*

TO LISTEN TO the story of Naboth is to feel, This is where I came in.
The history of our own time is marked by a long series of State
trials, with perjured witnesses, 'Sons of Belial', in plenty to say,
'He denounced the party leader. He is an enemy of the people.'
Sometimes, as in the trials of the Russian dissidents the victims
may be well-known, and the world looks on with helpless sympathy. More often the defendant is just another Naboth, some
poor peasant or factory worker or clerk who is dragged before a
local court, denounced and sentenced. Nor is it hard to give
similar examples of the repression of those who step out of line
from many countries, Right and Left, black and white, and of all
religions.

Tyranny has always in the end provoked a terrible retribution,
and no doubt it will go on doing so. Soon or late, in spirit if not in
the letter, the prophetic word comes true: 'In the place where dogs
licked the blood of Naboth shall dogs lick thy blood, even thine.'
But it is not about tyranny as such that I am asking you to think.
It is about a particular evil in human nature which makes it possible for tyranny to operate in this particular way, lulling the lazy
to sleep by posturing in a cloak of justice: I mean, the willingness
of ordinary people to tell systematic and deliberate lies. 'Set two
men, worthless fellows, before him, and let them bear witness
against him, saying, Thou didst curse God and the king.'

When you come to think about it, there is something deeply un-
natural and perverted about a lie. Here we are, with the miraculous power of our five senses and our minds, able to grasp what is

going on around us; and then, by the ingenious use of sounds or written marks we can pass on that knowledge to others, help each other, work together, bring happiness, pride, comfort. It really is an amazing and a wonderful gift. And then to use it to delude people, to waste this power on false and useless, even desperately harmful things – is that not perverted, despicable? It is just like using the gift of eating and drinking, which should bring life and health as a means of poisoning someone.

And for the Christian, there are so many other thoughts to take to heart on this matter. This power of ours comes from Someone, who meant it for our joy. What a miserable, hurtful thing to use it for mean, selfish and loveless ends. But God did more than just arrange for us to have this power. He used it himself. In his man's life, with all a man's hardships and temptations, surrounded by hatred and loneliness and danger, faced at the end by the threat of a terrible death, from all of which he could have escaped by bending the truth just a little, it is never recorded of him that he said one thing which was not straight and clear and honest. He came to show us the truth, and he did it to the end; so much so, that the writer of the Fourth Gospel could sum up the whole life of Jesus as God's own 'Word' made flesh.

Jesus himself underlined this in his teaching. In the Sermon on the Mount he laid it on the line: 'Let your Yes be Yes and your No, No. Anything more than that springs from evil.' Words, he is telling us, should mean what they say at all times. If we have to back up what we say with 'Believe you me!' and 'It's true as sure as I'm standing here,' we are admitting the possibility that some of the things we say may not always be true.

And when we stop to think of the other side of the picture, what a terrible lot of misery and heartbreak this evil causes! We started with a very dramatic example, that of the perversion of justice: countless men and women through the ages sent innocent to exile, imprisonment and death by perjured evidence. But what of the evidence which is not given in a court of law but over the garden fence, in the bar of the local, on a street corner or at a bus stop, between a nod and a wink and a 'You know what I mean....'? Where the lie is not put into so many words but is just allowed to happen. When someone's 'I wouldn't be surprised if...', or, 'I bet you anything you like if we only knew...' is passed on not indeed as a plain statement of fact but in such a way that the other person goes off thinking, 'Ah, they know but they won't let on...' We don't know anything of the sort; we never said we did; but we gave the impression, and so we lied. And somewhere somebody suffers unjustly – they lose a bit of trade, they are left out, a friend is hurt and ignores them, and they have no notion why.

Lucky they are if it is no more than that. There are lies that yield a more bitter harvest. Lies told by a public figure whose secret weakness has compromised him; lies told by a child who has played truant and fallen into bad company; lies told by husbands involved in crime or gambling, lies told by wives hopelessly in debt, lies told by youngsters hooked on drugs, until, when the truth comes out, the damage is almost past remedy.

Then there are the stupid, pointless lies that we hear every day and recognise for what they are. 'Oh yes, they came in fresh this morning...'; 'I never got your letter, it must have gone astray in the post'; NEW IMPROVED RECIPE which means CHEAPER AND NASTIER INGREDIENTS; or the pathological lying which is just sheer rip-roaring fantasy. We find this starting in children sometimes, and may think it amusing; but if they can't be weaned from it, it may have tragic results in later life.

All lying is disastrous in one way or another, and not simply because it misleads. It also makes personal relationships impossible. We see this clearly enough when we come across people, or political systems which use lying as a deliberate technique. These human beasts of prey rely on the fact that the first instinct in all of us is to believe what we hear – *especially* what we hear direct from another person's lips. The liar's purpose is served if the lie is believed for long enough to bring about the desired result. What happens afterwards does not matter. To cope with such methods we have to drop all our normal reactions and proceed by the most cautious calculation. In a word, we cannot treat such people as human beings; for our own safety we have to act as if they were an alien and dangerous species.

But in some degree all lying has this kind of effect, because it stops us getting to know the other person as they really are. We are dealing, whether we know it or not, with a sham, a dummy, a disguise. As Catherine Morland innocently marvelled to herself in Jane Austen's *Northanger Abbey*: 'Why he should say one thing so positively and mean another all the while was most unaccountable! How were people at that rate to be understood?'

How our heart warms to an open, candid person! We are prepared to put up with many faults for the happiness of knowing someone who is not afraid to trust us with their very self. That is why openness, candour and honesty are indispensable signs of true Christian fellowship; for the essence of life in the family of Christ's brothers and sisters, the sons and daughters of God, is that we trust each other with our lives and souls. 'Bear ye one another's burdens, and so fulfil the law of Christ' wrote Paul; and this cannot be done unless another piece of advice of his is taken: 'Putting away lying, speak ye every man truth with his neighbour.'

And last of all, surely it will be in a real fellowship that lying will be put away, because the reasons that drive men to lie are dealt with at the root. If we really value each other for what we are (as distinct from 'putting up with' each other in a spirit of so-called charity), then we do away with the need to pretend, to put on an act, to impress. (Social or intellectual snobbery can never have any place in the family of Christ). Perhaps nothing in this life can quite cure us of greed or fear, but certainly the hold of these motives is much weakened in a community where we are generous and ready to help each other in trouble, and where faith in the love of God and in his promise of eternal life is strong. Again, if we find God's world and his gift of life wonderful and help others to enjoy it in a fulfilling and satisfactory way, the need to lie to make life more interesting is cut at the root. And where forgiveness and forbearance are real and wholehearted, the fear that lies out of shame can be overcome. Such a community will know why the Holy Spirit is the Spirit of Truth, and will know by experience what Jesus meant when he said 'the truth will make you free.'

28 The Victories of God

Preached in St Margaret's, Westminster,
5 August 1979.

'With the weapons of righteousness for the right hand and the left' 2 Corinthians 6.7

WHAT ARE 'THE weapons of righteousness'? And do they really win any battles?

David would have said that the sling with which he killed Goliath was a weapon of righteousness. Partly because, as he firmly believed, Israel in that war was in the right, and the oppressive Philistines were in the wrong. But also for a rather stranger reason: that it was such a very inadequate weapon. Goliath was loaded with plate armour, and had a spear most men could not even lift. Our attention is also drawn especially to the fact that it had an iron head. All the rest of Goliath's equipment was bronze. This was the period in history which we classify as the transition from the Bronze Age to the Iron Age. Iron was harder and would take a sharper edge and keep it longer. Whether for tools or swords it gave the user a substantial advantage. Goliath seemingly was the absolutely up-to-date fighting man. David had five stones from the brook.

Of course we read the incident differently. With all the history of war to guide us we can see that the key to victory is firepower, and that it is the side which can kill more accurately and speedily at a greater distance which will win. Goliath's equipment was useless except at close quarters or at the limited throwing distance of his huge spear. David did not need to come within that range to strike the giant on a fatal spot unprotected by armour. Nevertheless let us stay with David a bit longer, and ask why he felt extra confident because he was so young, inexperienced and poorly armed.

The answer lies in an idea that runs through the Old Testament like a recurring theme in a symphony. To quote David's words to Goliath: 'The Lord saves not with sword and spear; for the battle is the Lord's, and he will give you into our hand.' Again

121

and again in the history of Israel we find the same thought. Victory is not just a matter of which side is the stronger. God fights for the side which he favours, and it is his strength which decides the day. David inherited this conviction from the time of the Judges who ruled before there was a King in Israel: Gideon, Deborah, Samson, all had won against impossible odds. Saul's son Jonathan did the same. And so it went on, after David, down the centuries, when Sennacherib the Assyrian failed to take Jerusalem, or when Judas Maccabeus, only 160 years before Christ defeated Greek armies much larger than his own Resistance forces. God does intervene, insists the Old Testament. It is his help that matters, and it is given to the righteous poor who have no worldly power.

When we come to the New Testament and the Christian experience, we find the very same words being used: 'Thanks be to God who gives us the victory' writes St Paul. But now, as he makes clear by the next phrase, the victory is 'through our Lord Jesus Christ', and it is a victory not in war but over sin, evil and death. Nevertheless the underlying thought is the same: *God* gives the victory, it is not something we can achieve by our own wisdom, goodness and strength. And he gives it to those who are poor, foolish, unimportant, and seemingly hopelessly ill-equipped. As St Paul puts it again: 'God chose what is foolish in the world to shame the wise; God chose what is weak in the world to shame the strong . . . so that no human being might boast in the presence of God.'

So we find victory going to those who use the seemingly feeble weapons of righteousness: truth, patience, kindliness, innocence of life, sincere love, gifts of the Holy Ghost, steadfast endurance. Or do we? Does victory really go to those who use such methods? Is that the lesson we learn when we look around the world with a cool and honest eye? You would probably say 'No', and I often feel like agreeing with you; but let me put one or two reflections on the other side.

First, do the weapons of *un*righteousness really win any victories at all? Of course they do, or seem to do, in the short term. But nothing they achieve endures. It is a lesson of history that tyranny and oppression provoke a revenge that ultimately brings them down in a welter of blood, unless through wisdom or indolence they relax their grip. Nor are they totally successful even in the short run. It seems to be a law of the human spirit that when independent thought and feeling are most ruthlessly put down, men and women are found who count not their lives dear unto themselves but must speak out, however hopeless the odds or terrible the cost. There is a precious cussedness about human beings which seems to ensure that you never get one hundred per cent compliance from any group of them on anything. You may call the objectors dissidents, subversives, deviants, enemies of the people, degenerates, any name you like; but if right is on their side, what they say and do will start harmonies vibrating in other hearts, and in the end you have a huge, swelling chord of criticism and defiance.

The ultimate futility of unrighteousness was never better illustrated than by the arms race today. The SALT 2 Agreement may prove to have been of use, when historians look back at the twentieth century, provided that it levels off the growth of nuclear delivery systems and so releases some resources for peaceful use; and also proves that each side can check on what the other is doing, and so prepares the ground for an actual reduction in arms next time. But the limits actually agreed are arrived at by the logic of lunacy. Each side seeks to have enough first-strike capability to wipe out the other side's effective missiles and still have sufficient in hand to 'win the war'. But the quantities needed for this preliminary disarming of the enemy would destroy all life on this planet anyway. So nobody *can* win.

Meanwhile the balance of terror, to which we owe the uneasy peace under which we live, casts its blight over the whole of life. We may not think about it much; but ask yourself this: if tomorrow morning the news broke that all nuclear weapons were to be dismantled and never used again would not the whole world look and feel a happier place? And what of perhaps the greatest corporate sin of our times, spending on armaments instead of on the urgent problems of poverty, health, food and so forth? The weapons of unrighteousness have doom built into them, doom for everyone.

It is the same with a subtler weapon, that of propaganda, or to give it its real name, lies. The effect of deliberate, systematic lying, or even just ignorant, prejudiced lying as the normal thing is to destroy confidence between human beings, to destroy community, and so to destroy people. Whenever a clash, or crisis, or cause of grievance arises, nationally or internationally, the public statements of the parties concerned are usually totally predictable. Anyone could write them out of the air with no investigation whatever. And since life is not that simple, and since the statements cannot all be true anyway, we know these utterances, nine times out of ten, are just standard-issue falsehoods. This verdict of commonsense is regularly reinforced when we happen to have access to the facts ourselves, or when later the truth comes out, so that gradually a huge cynicism becomes second nature.

Of course lies may go unchallenged if they are lies we want to hear. But even then their success is short-lived, because reality keeps contradicting them. One lie which is still being propagated in public life in this country, by industry, by labour, by Left and Right, is that we can all have a steadily rising standard of living if only we work for it – meaning that everyone can hope to have more and more sophisticated possessions and amenities. It simply is not true; and it has been known not to be true for at least ten to fifteen years. The carrying capacity of the world rules it out. Standard of living, as the consumer society understands those words, has got to come down in the developed countries. We ought to be turning our minds and energies to creating a good human life in the light of that fact, not repeating the lie like a magic spell. The weapons of unrighteousness always bring total disaster.

As indeed they do in individual life. The tyrannical father and possessive mother either lose their children or destroy them. Either way they waste and frustrate their own lives also. Those who habitually lie and deceive end up hollow and empty ghosts because they have no real relationships. Those who set their hearts on things and cannot live without them end up the pitiable slaves of lifeless, heedless objects that can do nothing for the deepest needs of the human heart. Force, manipulation, wealth, all betray us. The Devil is a cheat. He promises all and in the end gives nothing.

By contrast, the weapons of righteousness, though they seem limited, feeble, ineffective, do achieve something, and what they achieve endures. It is the good that survives: the achievements of good people, art and literature, the institutions of community and freedom – make your own list. They survive, their influence survives even longer, *because they evoke love.* Ordinary people love them and cherish them, and in doing so are changed for the better.

So too in individual life. You can dragoon or manipulate people, and get results for a time, but they do not last. Take the pressure off and it all comes to nothing. But patience, truth, kindliness, sincere love, loyal endurance, these things make others better in their inmost hearts, so that they in their turn become creative centres of good, sources of life. The victories of God, like the Cross of Christ, seem pathetically small at the time but their effects are genuine, and they are beyond our calculation.

29 Good News to the Poor

'The Good News is preached to the poor'
St Matthew 11.5

WHEN JOHN THE Baptist was in prison, and seized by doubt and depression, he sent two of his followers to Jesus to ask him: 'Are you really the One who is to come from God or are we to wait for someone else?' Jesus's answer was that the messengers should go back to John and report not some personal claim by Jesus but the evidence of their own eyes as to what was happening. There were clear signs which showed that God was at work through Jesus: 'Go and tell John what you hear and see: the blind recover their sight, the lame walk, lepers are made clean, the deaf hear, the dead are raised and the Good News is preached to the poor.'

Does not that list strike you as in one respect just a little bit strange? It is meant to be a list of miracles; and in particular of miracles which the Old Testament had foretold would happen when God brought in the age of salvation on the earth. Jesus is obviously saying, 'This is God's promised Time. It is here, it has already begun.' But is it not a bit of an anti-climax to put at the end of your list of signs that God is at work: 'the Good News is preached to the poor.' Miracles of healing are one thing, but what sort of miracle is this?

The Church spends much of its time preaching. Not just from the pulpit, but in books and newspapers, on radio and television, in schools and colleges and institutes of adult education all over the world it strives to put across the Good News of the Gospel. Now this is quite a difficult job, certainly difficult to do well. But surely it is not a miracle? It calls for good sense, imagination, careful thought, and sensitivity to the needs and situation of the particular audience. But these are only the qualities every teacher has to have when teaching any subject effectively. As for saying that it is a miracle that it should happen at all, that the

126

very fact that an organisation tries to put across its message is a sign that God is at work, that surely is something of an exaggeration?

But Jesus did not say merely: 'The Good News is preached' – he said, 'the Good news is preached to the poor'; and it is in those last three words that we shall feel the bite, if we are sensitive. Let us think about them a little, and perhaps we shall see that it does take a miracle of grace to make them come true, and that where they do, God is very manifestly at work.

Who are the poor? First and foremost, those who have nothing. We talk nowadays about the 'poverty line' and the 'poverty trap'; meaning that there are people in our society whose incomes have fallen well below the average, or who by odd quirks of arithmetic are actually made worse off by the very measures designed to help them. God forbid that one should even seem to make light of the hardships and difficulties of such people. But their position, however hard or worrying, is not that of the poor in the absolute sense of that word. Between the states of having something and of having nothing there is a great gulf fixed which no effort of mere imagination can cross.

To have something – be it only half of a barely furnished room, one change of clothing, and a menial part-time job – is to have a toe-hold on the cliff-face of existence, the chance, however slim, to do something for yourself. It is to be able to look other people in the face because at least you have a right to whatever you do have. It means you can genuinely give something to another human being, even if no more than a half-cigarette or a cup of tea out of the pot. Such people may be angry or bitter, weary or resigned; some manage somehow to be happy. But, whichever it may be, they are still their own man or woman; they know that they exist in their own right.

But to have nothing; to be totally dependent on others, on charity voluntary or official, on what you can beg – or steal, – that is to exist only by courtesy of others. It is to have no significance whatever, to feel in your bones that you are a non-person. And what Good News do you preach to such as these? And how do you preach it?

Generally speaking, we don't. You will not find in church the sort of people who sleep in the doorways of Central Hall across the road. And if we tried to preach to them, what would we say? That there is hope? Pick yourself up, and try again? Your sins are forgiven? How can someone who is nothing feel responsibilities to his fellow-men? and if he cannot feel responsibility, how can he have any sincere awareness of sin? He can only pretend to have it in order to please the pious who want to help him. In other words, how do the standard phrases of Christian piety convey any meaning to the totally poor?

And yet the state of utter poverty is also a parable of all human existence. For, whatever we may like to think, none of us in the end are anything permanent in ourselves. What we are, and even our limited power to make something unique of what we are, we owe to others, and in the end to God; and without God whatever we make of ourselves must one day fall into nothing. It is because the state of the totally poor is a picture of the ultimate truth about all of us that some of the greatest saints have been able to take up the life of total poverty and make it a shining demonstration of joy and trust in God and of love for their fellow men. For what Jesus said when he preached to the poor was not: 'Oh dear, you have got yourself into a mess; but, never mind, if you try and turn over a new leaf God will help you out of it', but: 'Blessed are you who are poor, for yours is the Kingdom of Heaven.' That has some right to be called Good News.

Well that may be so, but does not common sense revolt at it? Are we to leave the poor in their destitution? Of course not – and from the earliest times right down to our own day, with its heroines like Mother Teresa of Calcutta and her sisters, Christians have been found among those helping the poorest of the poor back to dignity and a better life. But they have been able to do this work, often when society as a whole passed by on the other side, precisely because of this vision. If it be true that, whatever our wealth or education or human status, we are all the poorest of the poor in our relationship with God; and if nevertheless that relationship is true blessedness, because God loves us as we are, and gave his Eternal Son to share this poverty-stricken life of ours; then we can have no feelings of superiority toward the poor. We are not stooping to help them out of our generous abundance, not trying to make them as good as ourselves. In everything that matters in eternity they are as good as we are – more so, perhaps, if we are blind to our own poverty and dependence. And only on that basis can we really help them, or find words that will mean something to them, because we are then bringing them God's kind of love, not our own.

In conclusion, a more general reflection. If the Good News of God's love in Jesus is true, it is true for everyone. And that includes the rich and powerful and educated, as well as the poor. This, after all, is one enormous difference between the Christian and the Marxist. The Marxist also says, in his own way, 'Blessed are you poor'; but to him this means setting the poor against the rest as their enemies, resolving the problem by conflict and confrontation. As someone said to me this week: 'The logical end of that journey is always the gun.' The follower of Christ knows this is wrong. The end of his journey is always love, joy, peace, fellowship.

But there can be no bringing men together in this way until we realise that we are all poor, all of us, however much money we have, however clever or important we may be. 'The Gospel is preached to the poor' – and only to the poor, because only those who know themselves to be totally poor can hear what it is saying, and find true blessedness in that poverty which depends wholly on God's eternal love. When that Good News really takes possession of our inmost soul, then a quite new kind of love and brotherhood toward others flows from us; and then it is not we who help them, but God who helps them through us, and us through them. And that help is worth having.

30 The Powers of Good

WE HAVE BEEN having some beautiful days lately. The other morning, on the way to Matins, I was astonished to see one of my venerable colleagues break into a trot and spring lithely up six steps. 'You look jolly fit!' I said. 'Well', he replied, 'it's the sort of morning that helps.'

And indeed it was. Yet I dare swear there were some poor people about who hadn't really taken in what it was like. You must have had it happen to you that you say to someone, 'Isn't it a lovely day!' and just for a second a startled look comes over their faces as they wake up out of whatever thoughts or feelings were preoccupying them, and suddenly realise that, yes, it is a marvellous day and they hadn't been taking a blind bit of notice. It is so easy to live entirely inside yourself, aware only of your aches and pains, your worries, grievances, failures, your plans and daydreams, and pay no attention whatever to what is going on around you. Most of us are guilty of this at one time or another, sometimes very pardonably when we have big worries or feel ill and tired. But it can become a habit, something we fall into with no adequate excuse; and that is very sad.

Just to be awake and aware, then, is a good thing, a step forward. If we are alive let us live! But this is very far from the whole story. We can, if we will, learn to be aware of things in a deeper way and with larger meaning, so that our whole life is changed. To acknowledge the beautiful day is a start. The next level is to respond to it, as my friend did, by being happy, by putting a spring in your step, by tackling life with new faith, hope and love, because somehow anything else would seem ungrateful, a bit of an insult to such a glorious world.

But if we are at all sensitive to the life around us we are not going to stop there. It will not be good enough to respond as if we were the only person on the face of the earth. We shall be aware of those for whom it is not a beautiful day, who are not in a position to respond to it. The blind, who cannot see the sun; those confined to their room who cannot feel the air; those weighed down by grief, for whom the day, just because it is so beautiful, seems a particularly cruel mockery. The circle of our awareness, you see, grows wider. First, just the day in itself then, the day in relation to ourselves; then, the day in relation to other people.

And there we might well stop, with a confused and confusing mystery on our hands. The splendour of the day has brought us once more to an awareness of what some people feel is the last word we can say about the world: that it is an inextricable tangle of good and evil, and one has no more significance than the other; that both are hard facts, and we just have to accept them as there, without trying to explain them or solve the puzzle. It is true, I think, that good people, including good Christians, often shy away from facing the real nature of evil, from seeing the question it sets us. It is very easy to think that the kind of things we call 'evil' are surface matters, mistakes we can learn to put right, and then all will be well in a basically good world. Just as diseases can be prevented, illnesses cured, hunger fed, ignorance educated, so everything that spoils human life can be remedied if the will to do so is there. This is not to make light of the evils – those who think this way by and large are sensitive and serious people. Nor is it to deny guilt – on the contrary, by insisting that matters can be put right they emphasise how guilty we all are to let them go so wrong. Nevertheless, I repeat, the real challenge of evil is not faced.

The challenge is this: that evil seems so much part and parcel of the very stuff and fibre of things. The liability to disease is built into the nature of organic life; the infliction and enduring of pain is built into the animal kingdom; the deviation of sin in the lust for power, pleasure and individual self-fulfilment is built into the human race; and transience and death are built into everything. Just as no regimen, however healthy, can guarantee freedom from some form of breakdown or malfunction in our bodies, so no laws nor educational systems can protect a civilisation from conflict, tyranny and decay. Cure one social evil and another springs up to take its place. Evil itself is more deeply rooted and persistent than any particular evils. It seems almost inbred.

The other day Bishop Edmund Robert Morgan died. He had been the principal creator of the College of the Ascension, Selly

Oak, the great Anglican missionary training centre of the '20s and '30s, and later, as Bishop of Truro, one of the best loved diocesans of the Church of England. Let me quote a few lines from his obituary: '... he was to suffer the grievous loss of two of his sons in the war, but this great blow only seemed to deepen the simplicity of his faith. "Religion," he said once, "is simple. We make it hard for ourselves, but really it is only trusting in the goodness of God." But he knew himself the sacrificial cost of it.'

'Religion ... is trusting in the goodness of God.' In saying that, Bishop Morgan was following simply and directly in the steps of his Master – for what else does it mean to call God affectionately 'Father' as Jesus taught us? and did not Jesus too hold to that at sacrificial cost all the way to Calvary? 'Religion is trusting in the goodness of God.' But if religion is true, if that trust is well founded, if God really is good, then it is not enough to be aware of life simply as a complex interweaving of good and evil, of dark and light, death and life locked in an unending combat which may sway now this way now that but can never finally be resolved. We have to see good and evil differently. We have to be aware of everything that is good not just as good in itself but as the power of God and both a sign of his ultimate victory and a means toward it. Our lovely day is more than just a lovely day. It is the grace of God enlightening, enriching and strengthening our lives; and we do not see it for what it really is unless we are aware of it also at this fourth, this deepest and largest level, in relation not just to other people and the world, but to God.

This way of seeing things, this level of awareness, applies to everything that is good: the support of friends, the love of husband or wife, the kindness of a stranger, the beauty of art and music, the skill of the craftsman, the helpful order of a great civilisation, the affection of animals, health of body and mind, the taste of good food and drink, the sparkle of good-natured fun shared with relaxed and congenial companions. Those are just obvious examples; the possibilities are legion. I was once in a group which was asked to compile a list of the things in life they could honestly thank God for which had come into existence only since 1945 – and between us we ended up with seventy-three different items! And we have not mentioned the good things that arise from the actual struggle with evil: courage, forgiveness, compassion, reconciliation, and so forth.

We need urgently, each one of us, to be aware of all these things – to cultivate awareness of them, for too often we miss them altogether. And we need to be aware of them not as entries in a credit and debit account, which are cancelled out by the bad things on the other side, but as the creative power of God which gives us the strength and faith to triumph over the bad things.

In a television programme some time ago a Church Army Sister was interviewed, and in response to one particular question said something like this: 'I do understand just how St Paul felt when he couldn't decide whether it would be best to die or to live. It would be marvellous to die and to be with Jesus for ever, but life here is so wonderful and there is so much to do, I just can't make up my mind. I shall have to leave it to God.' The point of the story being that the woman who said that was in bed and ravaged with cancer.

The good in life is so very much more than just good. Evil is strong, with a brute, tyrannical force that destroys without pity. But good has an immortal, resurrection power that does not merely eliminate its foes but transforms them into means and occasions of good. This is the real war to decide the outcome of history and it goes on all the time. With every moment of truth, beauty or goodness a spiritual warrior, armed with God's pure and life-giving weapons, enters that battle; and when we welcome these as our allies and guardians we do indeed 'entertain angels unawares.'

Four months before his execution by the Nazis, at New Year, 1945, Dietrich Bonhoeffer wrote a poem, the last four lines of which I leave with you as one very important message of this season of St Michael and All Angels:

> 'While all the powers of God aid and attend us,
> boldly we'll face the future, come what may
> At even and at morn, God will befriend us,
> and oh, most surely on each newborn day!'

31 Love

THERE ARE TIMES when one longs for a ban on some particular word which is being worked to death – or perhaps not 'worked', just mouthed unthinkingly as a panacea for all ills, a key to every problem. In social, industrial and political affairs the word 'participation' has recently been having a run in this role. In Christian circles the current catchall, save-all has been in vogue rather longer, and has a more respectable ancestry. It is, of course, our old friend, LOVE.

Love has always been a part of Christian theory, and often, thank God, of Christian practice in the lives of millions of God's friends, known to us and unknown. But of recent years it has been made to bear the burden and heat of the day virtually on its own. Why is this?

Some of the reasons are purely secular, because we are all children of our own time – and a good thing too, for otherwise the Gospel would never make contact with today at all. Our culture is conscious, through popularised psychology, of the damage that lack of love can do, of all those people crippled and distorted in their personal lives by having been denied love or the showing of love. We are aware too of the vital part played by acceptance in rescuing people from anti-social or addictive patterns of life. Again, the whole field of personal morality is in chaos; and we turn to the notion of love, however vague or elusive it may be, to give us our clues as to the right thing to do. Society makes these demands on love, and we can hardly help going along with them.

But Christians also have their own reasons, very fundamental ones, for focussing on love. These reasons are connected with the difficulty and uncertainty of belief today. When St John wrote, 'God is Love', the overwhelming majority of people in his world had no doubt at all that beings called 'gods' existed. What blew their minds, if they were pagans, was the dazzling idea that there was only one such being, and that the character of this God could be summed up as Love. That really was Good News, because it gave them a new and total assurance that in essence life was good, that there was no need for fear or despair. They were released for joy, boldness, generosity. Today that Gospel has no such effect, because in a scientific age the popular world-view has no room for God. So we react in two ways. If, against the current of the world, we still believe in God, yet we feel that the only way to keep the lines open to him for others is to create in the world more of that Love which he is, so that life itself may become a more credible witness to him. And if we doubt, then the vision of Love as the true secret of living is the one thing we can salvage from the wreck and which no one can take from us.

A rather similar thing happens in our attitude to Jesus. If we believe in him as God Incarnate, as I do myself, we may still feel that this belief cannot be commended today simply by appealing to the evidence of his miracles, or of things he is reported to have said, or supremely, of his Resurrection – which was once the standard approach. We need to present him as the supreme and unique incarnation of Love; and to vindicate his Spirit as a living reality today by the sovereignty of Love in our own lives. And if we cannot accept him as anything more than a man, then it becomes even more important to justify the claims we make for him as *the* Man par excellence by that standard of Love which our contemporaries value so highly.

This centrality of Love is underlined by the two great commandments in which Jesus saw the crux of Old Testament teaching: 'Thou shalt love the Lord thy God with all thy heart and with all thy soul and with all thy mind and with all thy strength, and thy neighbour as thyself.' To part of what they saw we nowadays respond readily. Take, for instance, the command to 'love your neighbour as *yourself*'. We understand now, better perhaps than earlier generations, the deep sense in which it is absolutely vital that we should love ourselves. Tens of thousands of people are in mental hospitals, hundreds of thousands more drag out their lives, a misery to themselves and the rest of the world, for no other reason than that underneath, quite unconsciously, they hate and despise themselves. Like a subliminal tape-recording part of them goes endlessly on, criticizing, condemning, taking out its fears and resentments in crippling denigration: 'You're a failure, you're hopeless, nobody could like you, you're not fit to live.' Many victims can get by only by projecting this hatred on to others. They see no good in anyone; the whole world is corrupt, unreliable, selfish, cruel. Those who do not love themselves assuredly cannot love others. But why do people get like that? Because they themselves have not been loved. The whole thing is a bequest of evil, a doom handed down from one generation to the next. I am not loved; I cannot love; so those dependent on me for love cannot love either. 'Loving your neighbour as yourself' sums up the whole network of mutual dependence which is what human life is all about.

But what is the essence of this loving? Here again the Old Testament can help us. It comes as a bit of a surprise to learn that the background to the word 'love' in Israel's religion may not simply be that of private personal relationships. Those are the situations from which we normally read off the meaning of love; but in the world of Deuteronomy, for example, the word also reflected the political allegiance of a subject to his overlord. To love is to show steadfast loyalty, whatever the seductions or difficulties. And to this idea too we ought to be able to respond. For unshakable loyalty is the one thing that creates security, enabling a child to grow, the psychological victim to find a way back. Loyalty it is which alone forgives to seventy times seven, loyalty which knows how to speak the truth in love, loyalty which trusts enough to let others be themselves.

These two commandments had been identified as supreme in the Old Testament Law before Jesus came. He was giving his support to an insight already attained. But it was entirely in keeping with what else we know of him that he should have done so. These are the two commands on which all the others hang because they express the basic commitment the others exist to serve – commitment not to this or that ideal or duty or piece of behaviour, but to persons. Rules are there to help us live out our loyal devotion to the good of our fellow beings, and for no other purpose.

But there is one thing we are in danger of forgetting. There are three beings we are commanded to love, not two: not just our neighbour and ourself but also God. He too, he above all, is to be the object of our loyalty, our acceptance, our trust. This is not an easy command to keep. There is enough ugliness, evil and pain in the world to shake our trust, to snap our loyalty, to choke off our acceptance, and so to make us doubt the existence of a God worthy the name. Only one thing, so far as I can see, could make it possible to keep this command; and that is that God himself, without ceasing to be God, should truly and authentically have shared our struggle with pain, evil, ugliness and death. For me, if God has not done this, then there is no God. But in Jesus, as I believe, he has done it. There the infinite love has set us free to love him and to trust steadfastly in the ultimate rightness of things.

32 Letting go

Preached in the London University Church of
Christ the King, 16 October 1977.

*'And I say to you, my friends: Do not be afraid of
those who kill the body, and after that have no
more that they can do. St Luke 12.4*

IN FLORENCE, IN the Church of Santa Trinità, just to the left of the
High Altar, there is a slab in the floor carved with these words:
'*Viventes spe mortis, mortui spe vitae fruuntur*' – 'The living enjoy
the hope of death, the dead the hope of life'. Neither part of the
epigram is a sentiment you hear voiced very often to-day – even,
be it said, among Christians.

We live in a dangerous world, but one whose dangers have
become in recent times more and more paradoxical. For people
like us, life has never in all recorded history been less dangerous.
The figures for average expectation of life prove that. And the
same is beginning to come true (though far too slowly and for too
few) in less pampered parts of the world. But this very fact starts
the pendulum swinging back toward more danger; for it means a
world in which there are too many people, and too many of them
(especially in the rich societies) old and feeble and slow-witted,
not much use either for work or for war. If there is no effective voluntary solution to the world population problem, then your generation may well see it resolved either by the culling method of
global conflict or by forcible restriction of numbers. It will not
then be a matter of fighting for the right to abortion or euthanasia when you want them, but of having to submit to them when you
don't want them. Survival situations have a way of making a lot
of fine-drawn ethical arguments seem pretty irrelevant.

But why, we may wonder, should there be any need for coercion? Why should not the end of life be like a group of children
playing, who have, let us say, just the one bicycle or pony or
toboggan between them, so that after a time one will say to the
next, 'Here, I've had my turn; you have a go now'? After all, and I
address the question to myself as a professing Christian – if I

138

really believe in eternal life beyond the grave, would this be such a hardship? Would it not in fact be a sign that one had used one's life to reach a spiritual maturity that one was ready to do this? Even to suggest the idea as an at all general possibility is to court derision; and that says something about the degree of reality in our religious belief. For it is not always true that such beliefs have so little cutting edge. In Shanghai between the wars, if you had the ill luck to be condemned to death, it was quite often possible for a sum of money to find someone to take your place. Quite young men of very poor families would volunteer in this way. The ransom rescued their kinsfolk from destitution, and they themselves were assured in the next world of the happiness that would come from the worship paid to the one who had saved his descendants.

But, of course, it is not just a matter of a rather thin and shaky belief in a future life. If those two words, 'no more' in our text, seem to come from a different, almost incomprehensible world – 'Do not be afraid of those who kill the body, and after that have *no more* that they can do' – the reason is not just that a new life beyond has become too speculative; it is that the satisfactions of this life here have become too imperative. The longer life and health can be made to last, and the more things there are to do with them, the more unhappy we become at missing out on any of the possibilities. This applies whether we are poor, and so feel understandably bitter that even the simplest of these blessings are not for us, or we are well off, and so are less pardonably aggrieved that we have neither the time nor the capacity to sample all the dishes on the buffet before us. It is our basic, unspoken assumption (whether we are secular or Christian seems to make little difference) that a man's life is in fact directly proportional to the abundance of the things – chances, experiences – that he possesses. Of course those who kill the body have no more that they can do. What more could there be?

Do not misunderstand me. It is no part of my argument to deny the prophetic call to social justice, or to discourage Christians from involvement in political action at community or national level, or in international affairs, to secure a proper access to the blessings of God's world for all the brothers and sisters of his Son. I still feel guilty enough, in the large and extremely comfortable house in the precincts of Westminster Abbey which has come my way because, in my case, the service of my Lord happened to co-incide with the needs of an Established Church, not to sentimen-talise over the spiritual dignity of the peasants of Bangladesh or the homeless of South London. I do not believe that the Church has ever been right to demand heroism as the method of first resort for achieving human goodness instead of the last, to con-centrate on exhorting men, women, yes and children, to be good in all circumstances instead of trying to make the circumstances conducive to being good. But behind all these blatant inequities, iniquities, will always rise the question-mark implicit in the words of Jesus: 'Happy are you who are poor, for yours is the Kingdom of Heaven'. And I do not think that we shall ever get our Christian moral and social vision right until we face that question.

If you ask me why I think this is so, my answer will be nothing on the face of it to do with morality but simply with belief. For Jesus's words are to do primarily not with social ethics but with belief. The Kingdom of Heaven belongs to the poor, because in the world as it is only the poor can accept the real God.

The world is, as we reflected just now, a dangerous world. There are dangers from Nature – disasters or the hostility of the elements – dangers from disease, dangers from our fellow-creatures, animal or human. As St Paul put it: 'perils of waters, perils of robbers, perils by mine own countrymen, perils by the heathen, perils in the wilderness, perils in the sea, perils among false brethren; weariness and painfulness, hunger and thirst, cold and nakedness'. And, to crown all, 'our sister, the death of the body, whom no man living can escape', death which, as St Bernard puts it, is the same for all, save that for the young it lies in ambush, while for the old it is waiting at the gate. What kind of a God could it be who was responsible for a world like that? What could his scale of values possibly be?

It would be a direct and superficially attractive answer to say: One who cared only for the life of pure spirit; who gave us the life of the body only so that we might learn to ignore it, who allowed pain and grief only so that we could come to rise above them. And some great religions have in effect said just that. But if that were so, what sense can we make of all the goodness and beauty of the physical order – the love we learn through the body, the powers of reason and the sense of truth developed by humble observation of evidence, the inward vision refined by the perception of outward beauty through hearing, sight or touch? Is nothing ever to be affirmed? Has happiness no eternal significance? Is it what it is solely that we may cancel it by training ourselves to renounce it without a qualm?

If we are to avoid that trap, then we must say that any plausible God must want us to realise to the full the potentials for good in his universe: by science and art, by justice and love in human relationships, by wisdom and care toward all creatures, to maximise joy. But to this the nature of things adds two riders. First, that joy can never be maximised if each rational creature devotes itself simply to seeking its own. At every turn we find laid upon us the task of bearing one another's burdens – laid upon us by the sheer inequalities between us: between old and young, parents and children, clever and stupid, strong and weak. Any gift, if it is to have its full effect for the increase of joy calls for sacrifice and self-denial in its possessor. And since the motivation for such self-denial, which cannot always be rewarded and often must go wholly unrecognised, is such things as love, concern, responsibility; since it will often hardly be possible without courage and forgiveness; we must assume that these qualities too would rank high in any divine scheme of things.

The second rider is this. That whatever love may dare, or wisdom plan, the task will never be fulfilled. The question therefore insists on an answer: is this simply an ineradicable flaw in the total scheme? and if so what does it imply? Is the truth of the matter that perfect joy and real love are logically incompatible (in which case Heaven is impossible)? And does that mean in turn that God himself, in any worthwhile sense of the word, is also logically impossible, and that our belief in him is but a brave attempt to make the best of a bad job?

In *Summoned by Bells*, Sir John Betjeman has a vivid line about life as a narrow path running round a sheer cliff-face in the mist. Between the rock-wall above and the precipice below to which our questioning has now brought us, there *is* a path, but it quickly vanishes ahead in mist and it is never wide enough for more than one at a time to walk along it. Whether we even spot that it is there depends on one thing: an intuition that the way to final fulfilment for the personality is not to escape from pain by refusing to love (which is suicide), nor to love and possess what we love (which is self-centredness), but to love passionately with mind, heart and soul and then to endure the pain of letting go (which is sacrifice). You will all know the lines from Tennyson's *In Memoriam*: '''Tis better to have loved and lost/than never to have loved at all'. You may not know Samuel Butler's parody in *The Way of All Flesh*: '''Tis better to have loved and lost than never to have lost at all'. Each had half of the right, but I fancy Butler's may be the profounder half. For if there is a path through the mist of the world, this is it. If there is to be fulfilment, a way to solid and unending joy for everyone, then this pattern of loving and letting go, first in small ways, as with parents and their children, finally in letting go life itself, is the only one that our world of Time and Chance and Death has room for, and that the God of such a world could have intended.

A strange God, and hard for us to accept, precisely because we find this pattern of loving and letting go itself unacceptable. Yet there are clues to such a God, for example in our having the very margin of freedom which enables us to reject the pattern; for that freedom could be the God who loved us letting go. But the strongest clue of all was One who loved men and women, and spent himself for the increase of their joy, who loved life but let it go rather than betray what he had lived by, and whom God raised from the dead.

Nevertheless, even if we see in this mysterious event a clue to God, is there not still an ambiguity about it? If Resurrection is simply God's reward bestowed from outside on those creatures who submit to sacrifice, then there is still no intrinsic moral meaning in the world, because there is no organic unity between the fulfilment and the way that has to be followed to attain it. God's created order imposes the way, but the fulfilment is arbitrary and from without. One thing could overcome this, and so far as I can see, only one: that the pattern should exist within God himself and be manifested by him within the world. That God in his Eternity should love and yet let go the very Heart and Image of his Selfhood, and that within the terms of the world that divine Selfhood should also love all to the uttermost and let all go. So we come back to the church of Santa Trinità and to our inscription. For the poetic symbol of the Holy Trinity is our clue and challenge to that mystery of letting go, of life through death, which is the only possible secret of goodness at the heart of the universe.

33 True Goodness

'THERE WAS A man in the land of Uz, whose name was Job.' So begins one of the epics of the human spirit, a work that stands alongside the supreme writings of any religion, the tragedies of Aeschylus, Sophocles or Shakespeare, the poetry of Homer, Milton or Dante. Yet it starts like a fairy story: 'There was a man in the land of Uz, whose name was Job.'

It is as well that the author begins so disarmingly, and continues in the same innocent strain, for the story he is about to tell is as horrible as any in the Old Testament. Reduced to bare details it tells how God authorized the killing of several hundred human beings and 7,000 sheep – and for what? To see if a kindly and honourable man of useful and blameless life could be induced to round on God and curse him. God is proud of Job – 'Look at that one', he says to Satan, 'there is none like him on the earth.' Satan shrugs cynically, and replies, 'They're all the same; they all crack sooner or later.' 'Not this one,' says God, 'and I'll prove it to you.' And so all these harmless people and dumb animals are wiped out for a wager. They are treated as expendable nonentities who can be obliterated without a thought simply in order to test one exceptional soul to destruction. What is the point of telling such a story?

The conventional wisdom of pious people, both in Israel and among her neighbours in the Ancient Near East, claimed that God, or the gods, looked after righteous folk. 'I have been young and now am old,' said the Psalmist, 'yet saw I never the righteous forsaken, nor his children begging their bread.' The Old Testament, and the writings of neighbouring peoples, are full of this theme, repeated with endless variations: Be good, and God will look after you.

'Why?' you may ask. 'Why did they go on saying something so obviously untrue?' Certainly not because they were unaware of the suffering in the world. Pain, disaster and death were part of

143

everyone's life then in a way we comfortable, protected Western people can hardly imagine. No, it was a question of faith. It mattered desperately to them to believe that God was good. Precisely because life was so harsh and humankind so weak, they needed to believe in an ultimate power active on the side of right, not of wrong. God, by definition was the 'High King of Heaven', and goodness in a King meant above all seeing that justice was done. To save us from the black hole of futility and hopelessness there had to be a God who would impose justice on the brutal chaos of human life. That faith could indeed be so strong in them that they believed it rather than the evidence of their own eyes and ears, and like the friends of Job assumed that anyone who suffered must be a sinner, whatever the appearances.

Such ideas may be superstition or wishful thinking, but we ought not to be too superior about them. Many, many Christian people today, in their heart of hearts, think that is how the world ought to be run, and half believe that is how it is run. How many times one hears the cry, 'Why did that have to happen to so-and-so? He was such a good man;' 'She was a wonderful person, it seems all wrong;' 'How can one believe in a God of love, when someone like that has to suffer so?' The lesson of life today as we see innocent families bereaved in Ulster or half a nation starving to death in Kampuchea seems plain enough. If there is a God he ought to be in charge and he ought to be good; so there is no God.

People felt just the same in ancient times. They voiced just the same argument. In Sumeria, in Babylon, in Assyria, over thousands of years they kept coming back to the old question: how can you make sense of suffering? Students were made to write essays on it. The most famous books about it became best-sellers. But only one has played a major part in human thought down the centuries: the Book of Job.

Yet the odd thing about the Book of Job is that it has been consistently misunderstood. We want it to answer that age-old question which is still our question: how can you justify the sufferings of good people? What answer can God give to a charge of cruelty or impotence? But to that the Book of Job refuses to give a reply. Bernard Shaw's famous jibe is in one way fair enough: 'If I complain that I am suffering unjustly, it is no answer to say, "Can you make a hippopotamus?"' – which is precisely what God does say to Job in the closing chapters. In fact God behaves badly throughout the book except at the very end, when he restores to Job the wealth, family and status he had so amorally taken from him. His so-called answer to Job is a hectoring, bullying exercise in which he merely keeps on shouting – admittedly in beautiful verse – 'You're not as big and clever as I am, so stop talking about things you don't understand.'

No doubt then as now many people dismissed the Book as a failure – a glorious failure, perhaps, but a failure all the same. But the only reason the Book of Job does not answer our question is that it is saying something much more important – and if we would stop and listen, we would realise that our question was the wrong one.

The key to it all comes in six critical words right at the beginning of the story: 'Does Job fear God for naught?' God may boast about his servant Job, but, as Satan points out, it pays Job to be good. 'Hast thou not put a hedge about him and his house and all that he has?' The really good person is the one who is good whatever the consequences. To be good when it always means health, security, prosperity, and every kind of blessing is not true goodness – it is just enlightened self-interest.

With that one question the Book of Job brings the whole worldview of the religious believer in the ancient world, and in many of ourselves today, crashing to the ground in ruins. A just God, a God who always looked after the good people, would make it impossible for us ever to be truly good. Is that what we want?

It really is very important that we should clear out of our minds, and help other people to clear out of their minds, the notion that if we are good, God will take steps to protect us and ours from illness, accident, crime, injustice, or death. Goodness may often bring happiness by simple cause and effect. But God will not intervene when it does not. Christ promised his followers many things but never security, success, and sunshine. How could we ever expect such things when he ended up, in this world, on a Cross?

God will not keep us safe and happy for being good because he has better things in mind for us – to be like Jesus, who was good whatever the cost. When we sing in a moment, 'Be thou my breastplate, my sword for the fight, Be thou my whole armour, be thou my true might; Be thou my soul's shelter, be thou my strong tower,' we are praying not for outward but inward strength and happiness – for the joy that comes from having God himself ever with us through good and ill alike, one with us in word and wisdom, one with us because, like Jesus, we are his true sons and daughters. Wealth and status are nothing – 'Riches I heed not, nor man's empty praise.' All that matters is God – 'Be *thou* mine inheritance now and always; Be thou and thou only the first in my heart; O Sovereign of Heaven, my treasure thou art.'

Yet we are still left with a difficulty. How can we feel like that about God, unless God is both good and very, very real? And if God does not rule the world in righteousness how can he be either of these things? The Book of Job has no answer to *that* question. It does us a vital service by warning us that, for our own soul's sake, we ought not to look for God to impose justice, but it does not tell us what to put in place of that. The trust in God to which Job wins through at the book's end is an act of purest faith.

The answer for which Job longed comes only in Christ. God's way of being good is that of sharing, of being one with the creatures he loves. We saw that victory has to be won from within, in the soul, that that is where true goodness begins. Well, God goes along with us, works the task alongside us, shows us, inspires us. He too endures the savage injustices of Fate. He triumphs over it, as we must triumph, by not allowing that savagery to turn him from what is good.

We can hardly blame the writer of Job for not foreseeing an answer so inconceivable as God sharing human life, the divine Word made flesh. We ought to be grateful to him for pointing us towards it, for helping us to recognise it when it is given: that God should be 'the great Heart of my own heart, whatever befall', and that only by becoming himself the 'best thought' and inward 'Vision' of all his children can he be truly 'Ruler of all.'

34 Marriage

Preached in Westminster Abbey,
22 October 1978.

*Let marriage be held in honour among all, and let
the marriage bed be undefiled; for God will judge
the immoral and adulterous. Hebrews 13.4*

IN ONE WAY it seems more difficult to preach about marriage
today than ever before. For is not the preacher in something of a
dilemma? To talk frankly about some of the basic problems
facing marriage today, in all the clinical detail that is now acceptable in lectures, books and discussion groups, is not appropriate
in the pulpit, and could well be a distressing and intolerable im-
position on many members of a congregation. Yet the preacher
who confines the sermon to moral and spiritual generalities is
liable to be dismissed as having nothing to offer to people's real
situations, since we are all of us nowadays accustomed to the
uncensored and factual approach.

But we must not let ourselves be trapped in such bogus choices.
Marriage in individual experience is an intimately personal
matter which demands to be treated with dignity and some reti-
cence even in the most private and confidential setting – and this
applies whether the particular marriage in question is happy
and fulfilled or deeply troubled and in danger of breakdown. But
marriage is also a public fact. Each individual marriage is a universal human idea worked out well or badly in one unique set of
circumstances. To that universal idea the Word of God addresses
itself, and is thus of direct and concrete relevance even though it
does not go into clinical detail.

The Christian vision of marriage is not an arbitrary set of
moral rules. It is perhaps the clearest example we have of what it
means to base your life on your belief about God and what he is
like. What, in the simplest possible terms, is the heart of the
Christian Gospel? It is that the eternal Son of God gave up his
divine life to share our human condition; that though his human
life was spent wholly in showing truth and love to his fellow

human beings they rejected and crucified him; but that, even so, such love could not be defeated – through and beyond death God gave Jesus back to us for ever, in an act of inexhaustible forgiveness and reconciliation. That is the pattern: sharing – love – rejection – forgiveness – reconciliation – life. Christian faith declares that this is the fundamental pattern behind the universe, the nature of God, the order to which we all must learn to attune ourselves if we would find our way to full and eternal living.

Now what Christianity has done, following the teaching of Jesus, is to take marriage, that natural, worldwide human idea and institution, in some form of which most human beings pass their lives, and to say: 'At its best, as it is meant to be, marriage is both a symbol of what God is like, and a means through which we can grow more like him, and so prepare ourselves to enjoy eternal life with him.' And the focal point of this vision is the requirement of mutual faithfulness 'till death us do part', each keeping only to the other so long as they both shall live. This mutual loyalty is completely unconditional. It is not a contract, which says: 'I will stay faithful to you, so long as you are faithful to me.' It does not say that, because God does not say that. Jesus remained faithful, even though everyone forsook, betrayed, reviled, tortured, killed him; God remained faithful even though his Son was rejected. Jesus's love was unconditional; God's love is not a contract. Neither must ours be.

In the marriage service the couple take each other, 'for better, for worse.' It cannot be stressed too strongly that this phrase includes the better and the worse in the marriage partner. The heartbeat of every marriage, as a Christian sees it, is forgiveness. It is true that Jesus set very high standards for his followers, in marriage as in many other things. But he did not commit the fatal error of most high-minded reformers, and make everything depend on success. He realised that we must have high ideals, that we must, for our soul's health, aim only at the best, not be content with the easy and mediocre. But he also realised that we all fail, and will go on failing at various points all our lives. So, again and again, as the central theme of his teaching he hammered home that this need not matter *provided* we are prepared to forgive and start again. 'Forgive us our trespasses', we are to pray, 'as we forgive those who trespass against us.'

Thus, a marriage, in order to endure, does not call for perfection in the partners, but it does demand a sincere and total readiness at all times to forgive.

This is a staggering requirement. Perhaps not in the case of two nice, well-adjusted, easily compatible people, who stay in love and also enjoy each other's company (not the same thing!) But most marriages are not like that, for the simple reason that most people are not nice, well-adjusted, open, adaptable, mature personalities. We have hang-ups, problems, deep fears and insecurities, prejudices that have been ingrained in us from childhood, unpleasant habits, fatal weaknesses. We may be sadists; we may be unable to show affection; we may be greedy, demanding, compulsive liars. But we fall in love, maybe with someone who is also physically infatuated and does not see through us, or quite possibly with someone who is unconsciously attracted to us because they suffer from the very same failings. A marriage is solemnized. And then what?

Then, some would say, the most exquisite form of hell on earth ever invented. What is the use, we may ask, of recommending forgiveness to people who need it precisely because they are the sort who are totally incapable of showing it? What can talk of forgiveness mean to those who refuse to admit they need it? who are always in the right in every argument? who say, 'Of course I shall go out on my own every night if I choose', or, 'I shall certainly have affairs if I want to; they mean nothing to me'? Where does forgiveness come into the picture with a couple who literally have not spoken to one another for years? What relevance can it have to those frozen in such a satanic parody of human relationship?

I don't know. Sometimes there seem no limits to the grotesque tragedies human beings can inflict on themselves. But I do know that it is treacherous special pleading to use such tragedies to discredit the ideal of lifelong fidelity in marriage for the majority of ordinary people. It would, I am sure, be wholly contrary to the spirit of Christ's teaching on forgiveness to withhold it from those who have come to grief in their marriages, some of whom have, for example, forgiven unto 69 times 7, and then given up in sheer exhaustion, while the only real sin of others has been that, perhaps very young, they have married when they were radically and dramatically unsuited, or when the fact that they would become so was not yet apparent, because their personalities were as yet only emerging. Failure in marriage must indeed never become the one unforgivable sin, whatever the circumstances. But the great majority of those who marry are not in these categories. They are people for whom lifelong partnership is perfectly feasible. And where it is feasible, it is a prize to be sought at all costs. If the Church believes this, it would certainly do well to give instruction to the unmarried on how to have the best chance of attaining it. We don't do that very widely, and that is bad. But the validity of the ideal remains.

People say, 'Getting married is a cage. We live together because we want to. If either of us didn't want to then it would be wrong.' What this totally ignores is the incalculable creative value of forward commitment. A child is free to develop without fear because it believes that its parents will never abandon it or cease to love it. That is why withdrawal of love punishments are so savagely destructive. And all of us, all our lives, need that security if we are to grow and mature. The believer finds it in God, certainly. But we all need that divine love given sacramental form in a human reality. (That after all is why Jesus came, is it not?) So far from being a cage, the marriage relationship is a liberation, because it promises us just this: a love on which we can rely. And those who have consolidated this by years of mutual forgiveness, appreciation and understanding attain a depth of humanity, a quality of living, which those who move from relationship to relationship, however serious or well-meant, never even suspect, much less experience.

One final thought. Because we human beings are such an intimate and inextricable mixture of body and spirit, what we do with our bodies matters in every aspect of our lives. Just as physical love strengthens the spiritual aspect of the marriage union, so physical infidelity weakens, and can destroy it. The husband or wife who defends infidelity by saying, 'It doesn't mean anything', is also saying that their physical love *within* marriage doesn't mean anything, that it is not really an expression of a spiritual commitment. In which case marriage becomes meaningless. For not the least of its blessings is that marriage integrates us by uniting body and soul in the service of a single loyalty. And that, ultimately, is the reason why the Church sets its face against full physical love with any but the marriage partner. The authentic vision is of the union of body and soul in a love that follows the example of God himself in loyalty even unto death. And that must mean loyalty now to the marriage which is yet to come.

35 Other People

AMONG THE LESS enjoyable episodes of life most of us would probably include that lonely moment when you walk into a big party or social function and you can't see a single person person you know. It's all right, of course, if you're the Lord Mayor or in the top table party; then someone rushes up to you, presses a drink into your hand, and wheels on a series of guests who are expected to keep you happy. But when you are just one of those almost accidental invitations, and no one really cares whether you turn up or not, it can be rather daunting. Everyone else seems to be having a marvellous time with old friends, and all you can do is stand there trying to look as though you don't mind.

So it was the first day at school, at work, at the university, in the Services. And so it could easily be the day we die.

There are, after all, an awful lot of people in the next world. We think of life after death as reunion with those we love who have gone before us. But they are a minute, almost invisible fraction of that incalculable host, that universe of souls.

And then, think how different from us most of them will be. In Italy once, speaking virtually no Italian, and running into difficulties, what a relief it was to come across a fellow-countryman and be able to talk about them! No doubt a good many of you have had the same experience. Well, we might as well face it: Heaven will be full of foreigners.

You think that is just a joke; and to some extent you are right. You may think it a joke in poor taste; but if so it is yet to a serious purpose. No doubt in the life beyond we no longer have to communicate in French or German or Italian; perhaps our thoughts are instantly plain to others without the need for words (which could be frightening!) No doubt, as many have imagined, we are met, as we pass between the worlds, and guided by angels, spiritual beings. We can hope that the faces we have 'loved long since and lost awhile' will be allowed to greet us and cushion the shock and strangeness. But in the end there are two facts we shall have to face.

The first is that in the land of the Trinity, where individuals remain themselves and yet are perfectly one with all other beings, the only distances put between us will be concessions made to our weakness by the courtesy of others more perfect than ourselves. And these concessions must be temporary. For in the end we must learn to be open enough to be truly one with all other members of the family of God. Only so can God's own Spirit, which loves all alike, dwell in us; and only if that divine Spirit is in us shall we have eternal life. Life everlasting, life in heaven, means life with others, intimately, totally shared.

The second fact we have to face is that these others will still be different. Many of the differences of this life will have gone, certainly – some were silly, some were sinful, others were a temporary necessity only. But no two people are exactly the same, not even at the deepest level of personality. A great part of the wonder and beauty of God's world is its variety. He actually can make things and people that are unique, and not only unique, but equally and uniquely precious. That multitudinous uniqueness, purified and perfect, is to be the glory of Heaven, the goal to which his plan has been working. If we are to have a place in Heaven we have got to be able to rejoice in everything that is *not* like ourselves. That is one of the main things which the Communion of Saints is all about. It is about differences made joyful by love. If the apostles from first century Bethsaida are to be one with the twentieth century products of Benares and Birmingham, to say nothing of those from other galaxies far beyond our reach, it will not be because we have all been processed into uniformity, like billions of identical sacred images moulded in clear acrylic resin. It will be because the peculiar excellence God has made out of each person's life story is so dear to all of us that we could not bear to lose a single one.

Now all this has a good deal to do with our life now. In all sorts of ways the wider world has started flowing down our street, slopping under our front door. People from Asia or the Caribbean move into the next house. French and Japanese buy up the firms for which we work. House agents' signs appear in Arabic. Directives hammered out in Europe tell us what we can and cannot eat. For years most of our popular culture has been a re-run of last year's fashion in the United States. Even in Church other Christians, of all people, burst in saying, What do you want bishops for? Why won't you ordain women? Why don't you speak with tongues? How can you be so silly as to baptize babies? 'Go away!' we cry, 'go away! For Heaven's sake, leave us alone!'

But, of course, it is precisely for Heaven's sake that they mustn't, because in Heaven it will all be a thousand times worse. But why should we call it 'worse'? Has not the Gospel been trying for two thousand years to make us see that what we call 'worse' is really much, much *better*? If it has failed, one reason is, I believe, that we practise our religion in ways unconsciously designed to keep everything strange, frightening or different at a safe distance. What we need is a spirituality for One World. We must learn to pray over the horizon.

By this I do not mean anything so trivial as up-dating our services, or introducing the news headlines into our intercessions. These are often little more than devices for keeping life at bay by pretending to become involved with it. Let me try to indicate the sort of thing we need by making two concrete suggestions.

The first is very simple and concerns self-denial. The heart of our faith is belief in a God who became one of us, who shared, endured, stood alongside. Can prayer really be the kind that springs from such a faith unless it is linked with some attempt, at least in some small degree, to share, endure, identify with the sorrows for which we pray? (I am speaking now to the comfortable, to those like myself who have more than enough.) Take giving – and I don't mean giving to the needs of the Church but primarily of the poor. Giving starts to be Christlike only when it starts to hurt, that is when we have to go without something *we* need. Jesus, you remember, rated the widow's mite above the lavish benefactions of the wealthy because they gave of their surplus while she gave her living. Only when we cut deep enough to take a corner off our living are we standing in any measure at all alongside the deprived. Again, we may not dress wastefully or ostentatiously, but until we have to go without a replacement that is really due, we are not sharing with the naked. We may not over-eat (perhaps we care too much for our health to do that!) but unless we fast, at least once a week, to the point at which we know the pangs of hunger, and then give away what we have not spent, our prayer for the hungry lacks seriousness.

The second suggestion is harder. It is that our prayer for 'all sorts and conditions of men' means very little unless we are prepared to be friends with people beyond the sorts and conditions with which we normally associate. The way to begin on this no doubt is to meet on neutral ground, perhaps in pursuit of some common interest. The opportunity may come through evening classes, through the Parents' Association at the local school, through helping at a hospital, through sport. It may come in the most obvious way of all – at work. But it will never be enough to be friendly only in that setting of common interest. The acid test of genuine friendship is this one thing: is your *home* open to the other person? Will you eat, drink and talk with them there, and go to their home for the same purpose, not as an act of charity, but because you value them as part of your life?

Nothing puts a more searching question to our unthinking scale of human values. Nothing challenges a family more – as many parents find out when their children make friends who do not fit what has hitherto been acceptable at home. Nothing challenges a Christian congregation more, when, for example, a traditional Western church finds a very non-Establishment Black sect two streets away, or when an upper middle class Anglican parish and a lower middle Free Church start probing gingerly at one another.

There was an old witticism: 'Hell is other people.' That is the exact opposite of the truth. Hell is being turned in on yourself or on a little clique of the like-minded. Hell is a world of separated individuals, frightened individuals, who therefore come to hate, to be callous and cruel, whose souls wither and die. It is Heaven which is other people, and the enrichment of life which comes from being open to them. To achieve this, the old counsels are still the best: self-denial in the cause of love; helping to carry each other's Cross; seeing Christ in everyone; behaving like the family of God; dying that we may be born to eternal life.

36 Activity of the Spirit

YOU KNOW HOW it is. You put the same camera into the hands of
two different people. Each of them knows which way up to hold it,
how to release the shutter without wobbling, where the sun
should be. But the pictures taken by one are interesting and attractive – not exhibition stuff maybe, but worth keeping, clear,
colourful, well-composed, and showing things you want to
remember. The pictures taken by the other person are a disaster.
If there is a dustbin or a bus stop within fifty yards it is sure to
dominate the view. Clothes-lines cut across the top corners, deck-
chairs push into the bottom ones, acres of foreground fill the
space and leave the main subject as if seen through the wrong end
of a telescope; or if it is in close-up, then at least a third of it will be
out of the picture altogether.

Why is this? Because these photographers are not really
looking at what is actually there in the viewfinder. They just
have a vague impression in their mind's eye, which they don't
stop to check against the reality. It is the same with drawing or
painting. If you have ever tried it, or had lessons, you will know
what a shock it is when you first pay attention to what things
really look like, and see that the roofline of that building is not
straight, though it was certainly built that way, but a long flat
curve, and that shadows are not all black or grey, but purple, blue
or green.

Looking, really looking, is an activity. It calls for effort, attention. That is why so much of the beauty in the world is wasted on
us. We are passive. Or preoccupied, chattering aloud to others, or
silently inside our heads to ourselves. We expect our senses to
work automatically. But they won't. So beauty, great and small,
washes over us, and makes no difference. To receive beauty we
must be active.

You will have noticed, too, how it is with ideas or information.
When a child is told something, the chances are that it will make

156

your life a misery for the next quarter of an hour with what in Parliament are called 'supplementary questions'. 'Don't ever stand under a tree in a thunderstorm', we say, quite rightly, 'you are more likely to be struck by lightning.' Then it starts. Why? How? How do you know? In the paper the other day someone was struck by lightning playing golf; he can't have been under a tree. No, but his club may have been metal. Trees aren't metal. No, but——. Well, why does lightning strike in one place and not in another? What is lightning anyway? Where does it come from?

By this time we are reduced to gibbering incoherence, most of us. But if only we were more like the child! Later on in life, when faced with an unfamiliar idea, or worse still, a disturbing one, we no longer behave sensibly like the child. We no longer ask for facts and reasons. We may try to argue, but if we are out of our depth, we soon stop. Nor do we go away quietly later to find out for ourselves, to mend our ignorance. Or, if perhaps we are impressed or convinced, we just think, 'How interesting!' and do no more. This applies particularly in church. Something in a lesson, or even a sermon, brings us up with a jerk, opens up new vistas. But we never pursue the thought, go back to find the glimpse, ask seriously what to do about it. So our lives are unchanged.

Thought, wisdom, understanding, these are all activities. They call for effort, attention; for courage to admit our own ignorance, and persistence to remedy it. That is why so much of the truth in the world is wasted. We expect it to stay and take root in us automatically. But it won't. So it makes no difference. To receive truth we must be active. You must often have thought sadly how it can be with personal relations. Often, thank God, they go very well. The world is full of happy marriages, united families, good friends. But how easy it is for things to go wrong! And if they do, how soon we can get into a situation where it seems as if nothing can be done to put it right. A child who has been let down at some critical point in life, and whose hurt has never been understood or even noticed, grows up into an adult determined not to need anyone. Or a child who for some reason has grown jealous or resentful may become unmanageable, testing the loyalty and affection of parents, brothers, sisters, uncles, aunts, almost literally to destruction. Great faith and patience and sensitivity are needed here, where too much severity or

157

strictness may be eagerly interpreted by the child as proof of the suspected rejection, too easy-going an attitude as indifference, while positive approaches often meet with nothing but petulance. It is wonderful that again and again time and commonsense do sort these things out. But not always, or sometimes only superficially. Then years later we find those sad souls who need to think that no one could ever really care for them; or the dried-up, twisted person who mistrusts all affection as just a ruse to get something out of them, all care and concern as a pose put on to impress outsiders or to make the benefactor feel good, or as a grudging duty done to satisfy conscience. Here, in this prison locked on the inside, we find the invalids who destroy themselves because they will not, on principle, do anything they are advised, and the neurotics who destroy others by years of putting the boot in on hearts that are breaking for them.

Even to be helped and cared for is an activity. It calls for a decision, an actual effort to trust, to believe in the good motives of others; the effort to open oneself, to be vulnerable and dependent by wanting help or asking for it; the discipline to rely on what is given. That is why so much of the love in the world is wasted. We think that if the love that is offered to us were really what it claims to be, it would do all the work on its own, dispelling new fears, healing our wounds, bringing peace, making it a pleasure to respond – how often this is the disastrous expectation of those who marry, for instance, without being ready for it! We wait passively for results. So love speaks, and we hear nothing; it embraces us, and we feel nothing. To receive love we must be active.

All receiving is also giving. We have to contribute something or we receive nothing. This is as true where what we receive is the grace of God as with everything else. If we will not open our eyes to the beauty of God's manifold creation, the beauty in the face of Christ and of his saints, look at it, attend to it as it really is, how will it ever feed and transform our feelings? If we will not exert ourselves to think, to face our ignorance, our fear of new and disturbing ideas, to follow up what is said to us in Christ's name, how can God's creative word make us anew? If we will not trust our fellow men and women, even in the Christian community, want their help, believe in it, rely on it, how is love ever to get inside us to break open our shell, make us grow, fulfil our possibilities? To receive we have to be receptive. That means an end to conceit, self-sufficiency, satisfaction with our safe little area of achievement. It means a readiness to face our own inadequacy.

We think of Jesus as the great Giver, the one who shows us the Father, brings the Father's love and forgiveness to men. But Jesus is a Giver only because he is first the one who receives, receives everything at God's hand as a sign of a Father's love, a Father's goodness, a Father's Kingdom. He learned, often in the teeth of contemporary attitudes, to see life that way by meditating on the realities of God's world, by facing the demands of God's word, and by opening his own heart to God's love. In prayer he received from God what in word and act he handed on to men. And he is as much our representative and example in the one as in the other.

In the Gospel we heard how a young boy offered five bread rolls and two grayling, and God fed a multitude. When we pray the Collect, 'Stir up, we beseech thee, O Lord, the wills of thy faithful people', we shall do best to think not of being stirred to achieve great things, but of being stirred to the simple act of will needed to receive great things. Of being stirred to look, to listen, and to be loved. Then God will see to the business of 'plenteously bringing forth the fruit of good works,' and to the reward that is to follow.

37

Advent

IN SOME WAYS, let's admit it, Advent can be a bit of an embarrassment.

It's all right having a special Christian New Year, an opportunity to make some new resolutions, or more likely renew some old ones. It's fine having a run-up period to Christmas, with the chance to prepare ourselves in spirit and not just in shopping for the Coming of Christ. But that brings us to the awkward part. Advent does not just look back to the First Coming of God, nor even around for his coming to our hearts in the present. It also looks forward to his Second Coming in an unknown future. 'He will come again in glory to judge the living and the dead.' We say it. In what sense do we mean it? There have always been people who have thought that one could work out the date of the end of the world from various clues in the Bible; that there would be an ordinary day, when the sun rose and the birds sang, and nature to all appearances was taking her normal course, and then God would intervene in dramatic and terrifying glory to put an end to it all. Do we think of it like that?

There can be no doubt that many of the early Christians certainly did. They expected Jesus to return on the clouds of heaven within a short time. So firmly did they commit themselves to this, that when it did not happen, their credibility was seriously endangered. The strain is showing in the Second Letter of Peter: 'In the last days there will come men who scoff at religion and live self-indulgent lives, and they will say: "Where now is the promise of his coming? Our fathers have been laid to rest, but still everything continues exactly as it has always been since the world began."' That phrase, 'In the last days', shows that the writer is still clinging to the official hope. In fact he uses the mockery and complaints as a sign of special depravity which means that the End is actually imminent! But we have to face it, those who thought as he did were wrong.

Why were they so sure in the first place? For many reasons, but chiefly for the same reason that there is a Christian faith at all: the Resurrection of Jesus. The resurrection of the dead was in Jewish belief something that was going to happen at the end of time when God would act to replace this present wicked world with a new one, his own Kingdom, in which righteousness would be supreme. When Jesus rose from the dead his friends and disciples took this quite naturally as a sign that the End was on the way. In St Paul's words, Jesus is 'the firstfruits of those who have fallen asleep.' The first fruits, the token of the whole harvest soon to come.

It was this understandable conviction that the End was at hand which also brought into the imagery of the Christian religion all the ideas of the Jews of the time about what that End would be like: war, famine, pestilence, earthquake, strange signs in the heavens, and finally the arrival of the heavenly Judge – in Christian belief, Jesus – seated on the clouds of heaven and clothed in divine glory, escorted by the armies of the angels. The kind of picture, in fact, preserved in hymns we still sing, such as 'Lo, he comes with clouds descending.' This was the way Jesus's contemporaries, with the Old Testament prophecies to guide them, inevitably thought about it, with the result that this picture became part of the New Testament, and so was regarded by later generations as sacred and infallible scripture, much to some people's embarrassment.

But it should not be an embarrassment, it should be an encouragement. For the first point to notice is this: the promise that turned out to be false is our strongest reason for believing that the heart of our faith is true. The vigour and persistence of this early Christian conviction that the End of all things was at hand is quite inexplicable unless they had the strongest reasons for believing that Jesus had actually risen from the dead. So let us be glad of that for a start.

Did Jesus himself predict an imminent End and his own second Coming? You might indeed think so, for why should they saddle him with a prediction that went wrong unless he actually made it? There is some force in that argument, but no more, I think, than in the opposite one: that they were so sure the End was coming that they could not bear that Jesus should miss the credit of having predicted it. The whole matter is very complex, and not to be fairly summarised in a short Sunday morning sermon. It is not even certain, on a careful reading of the Gospels, that Jesus was referring to himself when he spoke of the Son of Man as God's appointed judge at the last day.

What does seem fairly certain is that throughout his teaching Jesus urged men to live *as if* God were coming at any moment; and that he taught this not, as we might do, as a kind of mental exercise – 'Imagine how you would act if you thought that God might come in and catch you' – but because he saw it as built into the nature of reality that God, who is its supreme King, can call it all in at any moment he wishes. Indeed he went further even than that: he taught us to pray that God should come and establish his kingdom, whenever and however he wills – 'Thy kingdom come, thy will be done, on earth as in heaven'. This prayer is not meant to impose restrictions on God, as if the Kingdom had to be a rather more just and peaceful version of the world we already have. It leaves God his sovereign freedom; and it pleads with him to use it.

In the light of this prayer it seems to me, I must admit, very unlikely that Jesus concerned himself with subtle clues to God's timetable. The Kingdom of God was already breaking in as he spoke; and he sent the feet of his followers running down the roads of the world to wake men up while there was yet time. One recurring theme of his teaching is Time. 'Time, world, please', he seems to be saying. 'The time is at hand.' 'Watch, be alert, for you do not know the day or the hour.'

His disciples very naturally took all this to mean that the Day of Judgment was approaching literally as the prophets had foretold it. We need not make that mistake; indeed it is vital that we should not. If we really thought that the End was round the corner, and that it was going to take that particular form, there would be nothing for us to do but fold our hands and wait. But we do not know what the Day of the Lord is like, what forms the Kingdom will take as it breaks in. It is our job to watch and discern so that we are ready. That is the central message of both Advent and the Gospel: to read the world in a new light, because we believe in the breaking in of the Kingdom of God, and then to respond to our reading with energy and hope, born of trust in him who raised Jesus from the dead.

But have I not evaded the issue? Was Time really running out when Jesus came? Two thousand years have passed and how many more may not lie ahead, as Man slowly works his own purposes out!

I myself used to think like that; but now I am not so sure. Time is not absolute; it is relative. Think! How long did it take Man to travel from his beginnings to Bethlehem? No one knows for sure, but we are told now that recognisable ancestors of ours were on earth about two million years ago. Two million years from the beginnings to Bethlehem; two thousand from Bethlehem to now – and already we face a situation where the end of the human race is staring at us. You probably know Dr Martin Luther King's famous dictum: 'The choice for the human race is between non-violence and non-existence'. Nor is it only the frenzied momentum of nuclear war, germ war, chemical war, laser-beam war waiting to be unleashed. There are the demons of pollution, which we have created, slowly choking us; and the spectre of exhausted resources which we have raised by our greed and by our childish delight in the costly toys of civilisation.

To these perils only the human sanity of Jesus has any answer. Whatever the political and economic forms needed to give effect to it, only the peace and forgiveness, the renunciation of wealth, the love for enemies on which he insisted can create a spiritual situation in which there is hope for mankind. This is not some high-flown religious fantasy. It is simply human common sense; and all over the world ordinary people, who would not claim to be specifically Christian or even religious, have been recovering these simple facts of life for themselves, and proclaiming them in demo and song, in word and act.

It seems to me that there is more to be said for the New Testament perspective than the grave and learned scholars or the mocking opponents of Christianity realise. God's revelation and warning in Jesus had to be prepared for. Men and women had to be in a certain position before they could grasp its importance in even the smallest degree. But that meant cutting things very fine indeed. It may be almost two thousand years since Jesus walked the earth; but that represents only one thousandth part of our human history, the equivalent of one minute twenty-six seconds in a twenty-four hour day. And judging by how slow men have been to respond, by how criminally the Church has often falsified the message it was supposed to spread abroad, by how near we are to the precipice – don't you think perhaps God left it as late as he dared?

38 The Lively Oracles of God

A PIECE of advice sometimes given to visitors to Westminster Abbey is, 'Keep your eyes upwards and you'll be all right.' It is advice that dates from an earlier and happier time when inflation had not imposed such horrid necessities as entry fees, with all their attendant clutter. Today if you kept your eyes looking upwards you would almost certainly trip over a rope or knock down a barrier or crash into an electronic lightning-calculator ticket machine. Not to mention crushing the toes of numerous visitors from Tokyo, Rouen, Barcelona, Mannheim, Turin and Springfield, Illinois.

Still, the advice has its point. It is a great pity if you walk along the North and South aisles, for example, and see the memorials to Major André and Charles Darwin and to John Baker, Vice-Admiral of the White, and never give so much as a glance to the glory of the vaulting, thrusting up to the sky like the blades of young irises in spring. And what a waste of time it would be to visit Henry VII's Lady Chapel and never look at the roof!

All the same the idea behind the advice is not really a good one. It springs from an attitude of mind which regards all these hundreds of statues and memorials as merely third- or fourth-rate clutter, serving only to distract attention from the truly spiritual beauty of the Gothic building. This refined distaste is intensified by the sense that all these celebrations of a nation's very worldly achievements, of bloody victories in wars which, unlike those of 1914 and 1939, were often fought purely for gain or aggrandisement, have little to do with the Gospel or even with what is morally edifying. So what the advice is saying is really something much more far-reaching than how to get the best out of a quick trip round the Abbey. It is voicing a whole attitude to the past as such: that only those things in the past are worth bothering about which we happen to find sympathetic or inspiring.

This is today quite a widespread attitude. We do not go to the past to learn, but to patronise. When we read something rather good from Shakespeare or Plato or Goethe or Voltaire, quoted perhaps in the 'Thought for the Day' corner of our newspaper, we think, 'How clever of him to have said that all those years ago!' What is clever or admirable in the past is what we agree with, what we ourselves could have said, in substance anyway if not in those particular words. And, of course, by the reverse process we flatter ourselves, our own day and civilisation. By quoting and studying in popular culture, whether on TV or radio or in the printed word, only those ideas in tune with our own thoughts and dreams, we also build up a false picture of the past, in which all the really great minds share our own views. History thus doctored appears as a jerky but none the less fairly obvious climb up to our own lofty position.

Which is all very nice, but any number can play at that game. Marxists, Fascists, Liberals, Black Power, Humanists, Christians, and many more, all indulge in this futile exercise of selecting from the past those fragments – all taken out of context – which flatter their own conclusions. The one thing the past is never allowed to do is to criticise *us*. (It is an interesting thought, especially in a building as lovely as this, that the word 'mediaeval' is today a standard term of abuse.) We are all to be 'dragged screaming into the twentieth century'. It is perhaps the one sign of grace in the fanatics for all things modern that they accept that the natural reaction to being dragged into the twentieth century is to scream.

It is as silly, of course, to idealise the past and see no good in the present as to do the opposite. There has been much, very much in our century for which anyone of goodwill must give heartfelt thanks. What is sad is that we no longer believe seriously in the possibility of learning from the past. Perhaps the successes of modern science, both in theory and practice, have given us contempt for all aspects of less scientific ages. But that is very narrow-minded: for the deep realities of birth and death, love and hate, loneliness and relationship, good and evil, poverty and wealth, pain and happiness are always with us; and to assume that the good and wise of former ages, who were in many ways less shielded artificially from these things than we, have nothing to add, no different vision to show, no corrective to offer, is really very stupid.

This is a stupidity to which, you might think, Christians would be more immune than most. But they are not. They have, built into their faith and way of life, a huge cross-section of the past and its wisdom in the form of the Bible. For seventeen hundred years they turned to this as 'the royal law, the lively oracles of God'. But for the last two hundred, the period during which Western society has become steadily more contemptuous of the past, they too have grown more and more uneasy about the Bible. By now, it is hardly an exaggeration to say, they are split into two camps: those who still venerate the scriptures as inspired, and those who think of them as good in parts but in the last resort dispensable. And the views of each are made more rigid and extreme by those of the other.

Now let us be clear what is really sad about this. It is not sad that most Christians no longer think of the Bible as dictated word for word to chosen writers by the Holy Ghost. It is not sad that many no longer think of every story in the Bible as necessarily historically correct in all its details; or that we see many ideas as typical of their age and background. The Bible is truly a voice from the past, the real past. What is sad is that, having faced that fact, many Christians have therefore automatically assumed that the Bible can only have less and less of value to say to them as the generations go by. Its authority is not seen as different in kind perhaps from that which it had for their forefathers but just as real in its own way, but as something fading which will one day surely vanish altogether.

Christians now treat the Bible just as the newspapers treat Plato or Shakespeare, or tourists treat the Abbey. They look only at the bits which appeal to them, and arrogantly assume that these are the ones that matter. The first chapter of Genesis, or parts of Isaiah and St John, are the Gothic vaulting: that's all right, that's spiritual and eternal. But just as the sightseer today may sneer at the plethora of monuments to naval and military heroes, so the Bible reader will dismiss as unworthy or barbaric the stories of Joshua and the Judges, Saul and David, and their wars on behalf, as they believed, of God and his cause. But was not the writer of the Epistle to the Hebrews perhaps wiser than they when he included these men for their courage and endurance and self-sacrifice in the cause of God among the 'cloud of witnesses' which should prompt us to equal devotion and self-sacrifice in the far nobler following of Jesus? Again some, no doubt, as they walk through the cloisters, may feel superior when they spot the quaint epitaph to William Laurence, with the words, 'O reade these Lines againe: you seldome find A Servant faithfull and a Master kind.' What have we to do with servants and masters in these democratic days? So too the Christian, strolling round the New Testament, simply fails to take in the proper force of Jesus's words that he himself was among his own disciples as a servant and that so should all the chief of his followers behave to their bethren. Not 'servant' surely; let's say 'unselfish friend' or 'benefactor' or 'comrade'. What does not enter the Christian's head is that possibly he ought to let his own ideas be changed by those of the scripture, that he ought to think seriously what the word 'servant' meant when Jesus used it, and how that is most accurately to be lived today.

In all education what stretches the mind and increases knowledge is what we do not know, what we have never met before, the ideas that have not crossed our minds. Some of this will come to us from the present-day; but far more can come from the past, if we will but open ourselves to it. It all depends how you look at it. Of course, if you moan, 'What a lot of strange stuff! What good can that be?' then the Bible is just a problem, and the lessons in church that force you to listen to representative samples of it are a silly waste of time. But if you say, 'What luck to have all this from people so different from ourselves!' then the Bible ceases to be a problem, and becomes an inexhaustible adventure. And because the Bible is the work of people who were all, in their various times and different ways, wrestling with the mystery of God and how this world is to be known and loved as *his* world, the Bible then becomes also, for all who are prepared humbly to come to terms with it, the Word of God himself.

39

The Role of the Church

IT IS MORE than ten years now since I first read the Tale of the Eighteenth Camel. But I keep coming back to it as a parable which goes to the heart of so many human situations; and I would like to share it with you. (I apologize for the fact that you can't very well stop me if you've heard it before: that is one of the disadvantages of the sermon method!)

A certain Arab had three sons. When he died, he left in his will instructions about dividing up his property among them. Everything was quite straightforward except for the camels. Of these there were seventeen, and the will said that half were to go to the eldest son, a third to the middle son, and a ninth to the youngest. The sons had no more success than you or I would have done in dividing 17 by 2, 3, or 9, and ending up with non-amputated camels; so finally, in desperation, they went to a neighbour, an old friend of their father's, and asked his advice. The neighbour said: 'I have a camel. I will lend it to you, and you will find it will come out all right.' So he did; and, of course, once they had 18 camels, it was simple enough: the eldest son took a half, that was 9, the second a third, that was 6, and the youngest a ninth, that was 2, making (and this is the point) 17 camels in all. The neighbour then took his own camel back, and all was well.

There are many situations in life where we need to be like the eighteenth camel; and where serious trouble can develop if we are not. Two people, let us say, are having difficulties with their marriage, and they invoke the help and advice of a close and trusted friend. Such a friend ought to be like the eighteenth camel, there simply to make the insoluble problem come out, and then to vanish from the scene. But what can so easily happen? The friend becomes personally involved, the situation becomes a triangle, the stresses and strains are worse than ever, and finally comes a break-up which affects not only the two partners but the would-be helper as well. To argue, as people tend to do, that the marriage would probably have broken up anyway, may be true but misses the point, which is this: whenever we are called upon for advice or reconciliation our job is to help those concerned to find an answer to their present situation, not to create a new problem by intruding ourselves.

All professional counsellors, such as psychiatrists, doctors, probation officers, welfare workers, learn very early on that a solution which needs them as a permanent feature – a situation of dependence, or of transference – is no solution at all. In university work one regularly comes up against problems where students are in conflict with their parents: it is no good trying to help by injecting oneself into the situation as an ideal substitute parent, a dream-uncle, as it were. There is a temptation both to the counsellor to adopt this flattering role and to the young man or woman to treat one as such. Often in fact they come for advice precisely because unconsciously this is what they are looking for. But this only puts off the day when they must grow up and relate to their parents as people. Sooner or later the eighteenth camel has got to return to its owner.

This principle is not confined to such things as personal counselling. There are many jobs in life which we are doing well only so long as we are tending to put ourselves out of a job. This applies, for instance, to government. The task of government could be defined as 'creating those conditions in which all men and women can live in the greatest possible degree of freedom, security, and happiness.' Whatever political philosophers of the Left and Right have disagreed about, they have converged in their thinking on this: that in these ideal conditions the State machine should feature as little as possible. Thus, Karl Marx envisaged the ultimate withering away of the State; and the Book of Common Prayer prays, with perhaps more wistful yearning than genuine expectation, that 'we may be godly and *quietly* governed.'

Some individuals and institutions are concerned primarily with living – the butcher, the baker, the candlestick-maker, the artist, the scientist, the musician – others with helping people to live; and logically, the latter must in the end, if they do their job well, put themselves out of business. Once a baby is safely born, a midwife fades out of the life of mother and child. Once a psychiatric patient has worked through his or her problem, the therapist must quite the scene. So, too, those whose calling is to help a better society to be born or to resolve its problems ought, if they are to be successful, to be aiming at a situation where as governors and directors they can be phased out. Life and human nature being what they are, this is, of course, a goal we shall never actually achieve. But it is healthy for us to remember that it is the ideal, lest those of us who have this sort of responsibility come to think of ourselves as no less wise than God, and certainly more indispensable.

What Christians often fail to realise is that one institution meant to work for its own redundancy is the Church. The Church as such has no place in the final fulfilment of God's plan.

God's purpose all along has been the perfecting of his total creation. Within this vast design, which we cannot even begin to imagine, much less understand, we humans have been blessed by many acts of divine love, but above all by one in particular, the coming of God's own Son to bring new life to this world by himself sharing this world's life. This new life, as Jesus said over and over again, is one in which men and women know and love God as Father and each other as his children. The job of the Church is to plant this life so deeply in men's hearts that it becomes their natural outlook.

But if the Church were successful in this, it would, as the Church, be out of a job. That we have to talk about the Church at all implies that the Church and humankind are not the same thing, they are not co-extensive. If they were, we would not need to talk about the Church. Anglicans of all people ought to realise this, because the Church of England was intended from the start to embody the ideal that the Church is simply the State at prayer. Human sinfulness and perversity and that very definitely includes Christian sinfulness and perversity, make sure that this ideal never can be embodied. But it must be pursued. Once we lose sight of this, we begin to think that, whatever the world is like, somehow God ought to be satisfied because he has a devout following of religious enthusiasts. We, as it were, pat him on the shoulder and say, 'Never mind, Lord, you've got us!'

Christians exist for the sake of non-christians: that is the fundamental law of our being. Over and over again, in the tangle of people's relationships with God we are called in a multitude of situations to play the part of an eighteenth camel. If the mess were completely and permanently sorted out, we would all have the same owner, and the Church as an independent institution would fade from the scene. The Kingdom of God is the yeast in the lump of dough; but the purpose, as our Lord said in that parable, is that the whole lump shall be leavened. Or, as he said again, the purpose of salt is to give flavour to all the food. As salt of the earth, as servants of God's sovereignty, our calling is to avhieve these ends – not to turn everything into salt or yeast which would make life impossible, but to preserve God's world from corruption and make it into the good food of the spirit.

These thoughts may seem merely fanciful, spun out of an amusing story. But they are not. They run through the whole fabric of the Gospel. That story begins with John the Baptist, who was a prime example of what we have been saying: one whose whole mission in life was to prepare the way for someone else, to set up a relationship that would give men and women a life he himself could never give, and then to pass from the stage. Success for him *meant* making himself redundant. And what is the end and climax of the story, the achievement of One whom John himself testified was greater far than he? Was it not 'to visit us in great humility' that we might find our way not to him but through him to his Father and ours? Jesus is the world's Eighteenth Camel.

40 Silence

YOU MUST HAVE noticed. The most vital piece of equipment for today's young craftsman when starting on any job is a transistor radio. These marvels of modern technology are ubiquitous. People take them to cricket matches to listen to the commentators telling them what they are watching. They carry them on country walks – I suppose to make sure that nothing terrible can happen to them, like hearing the song of a blackbird or the chatter of the grasshoppers. But even the transistor is as nothing compared with that apotheosis of noise: the discotheque, the sole and supreme point of which seems to be to make sure that real pleasure runs no risk of being spoiled by anything so awful as human conversation.

Now I don't think there is anything really very new in all this. In the Twenties people shattered the peace of the Thames with wind-up gramophones in punts; and all over the world in every age noise, noise, and yet more noise has been the infallible method for ejecting demons and working off our human tensions. Technology has, it is true, added the risk of actual physical deafness, but the principle is still the same. It seems odd, nevertheless, that noise should be in such demand for pleasure, when there is so much of it in our ordinary daily life and work, and people profess to hate it so much. All of us feel at times, 'O how I wish this awful traffic would stop,' or, 'Not another jet!' or 'If only someone could turn that machine off for a minute!' Yet silence frightens us.

Silence can be a terrifying thing. Silence, you see, is quite different from peace and quiet. You can have peace and quiet over a drink with friends in a pub, or listening to records with your girl friend, or using up our energy resources driving out on Sunday. If you are feeling dreadfully ill, say, with a severe virus infection, but not delirious, to be left alone in bed, warm and undisturbed, that is peace and quiet. But suppose you feel all right; suppose

Silence

you are in hospital, in isolation, waiting for the results of crucial tests, perhaps in a darkened room wanting to know whether your sight can be saved, or immobilised after an eye operation: that is not peace and quiet, that is silence. And silence is not necessarily peace.

Silence is loneliness, perhaps the most acute form of loneliness there is. If you shut someone in total darkness for long enough, the brain will invent hallucinations because the absence of visual stimuli would otherwise drive them mad. In much the same way, if there is nothing to hear, babel breaks out in our head. Our own mind starts talking to us, frantically, in a panic. Of course, it says the first thing that comes into our head, so to speak; but that may be the very last thing we want to hear. Those fears, those anxieties, those feelings of guilt we suppressed so long. Those doubts about ourselves. They pop up on all sides. Then another part of us answers back, an argument starts, nervous and inconclusive.

Silence confronts us with ourselves. It makes our own self the only person to talk to. Our friends, let us say, have just left – it was a splendid party, but now the rather dreary room is empty. We are too tired to go to bed. Or perhaps there never is a party, but just a lonely drink around the corner, or a bite at the cafe, and then reluctantly home. And as the door closes behind us, the demons pounce. No wonder we turn on the wireless or the telly. Anything, so long as we don't have to think.

There is another sort of silence which is just as demonic: the silence between two friends or relatives or marriage partners who have quarrelled. How often over the years has one said to young people when preparing them for marriage: whatever you do, never sulk, never freeze the other person out, never put them in the doghouse! Whatever the effort, try to keep normal communication going; for once you lapse into silence for any length of time you will only carry on an endless, distorted, self-justifying conversation in your own head. This simply suggests a dozen new causes for anger, all of which burst out when you start talking again, and make matters worse.

Silence really tests out what we are. Only the honest and humble man or woman, only the man or woman who is not afraid, who needs no illusions to bolster the ego, only such a one can endure silence. Only the person who is more interested in the

173

world and in other people than in themselves can endure silence; for even in silence such people are taken out of themselves in wonder and love.

This helps us to understand also something that puzzles and distresses many Christians: the fact that not only do they find prayer difficult, but positively dislike it. For unless we are going to do nothing more than rattle off a number of set prayers by heart, we have sooner or later to endure silence. We have to give up ready-made noises, and simply concentrate on God in love, trust, and adoration, or on other people in love, and sensitive concern, or on ourselves, again with love, realistic, tolerant and courageous. For all these things we need silence, stillness, calmness. But as soon as we try to achieve this, all our fears, anxieties, resentments, frustrations rush out and start kicking up a terrible rumpus. And this is so unpleasant that we rapidly say the Our Father, jump into bed, and turn out the light. 'Prayer?' we later say, 'prayer? oh that's not for someone like me!'

There are ways of coping with these problems – indeed that is largely what meditation is all about – but they are not our immediate concern. What I would like to remind you now is that there was one man we all know about who was of that special sort for whom silence had no terrors. A man who regularly spent whole nights up in the hills, far from human habitation, six weeks once in the desert, in prayer to God. That man was Jesus. Our own experience convinces us that anyone who could do that sort of thing, not as an occasional gimmick, but as a necessity of spiritual strength and renewal must have been, to use our modern sort of language, extremely well integrated, free from fears and anxieties, trustful and positive in his attitude to life. The sort of man who alone with the heavens could call to God as 'Father' – and mean it.

Now Pascal, that great Christian thinker of seventeenth century France, contemplating the heavens – and how much they have grown since his time! – uttered the famous cry: 'The silence of these infinite spaces terrifies me!' And so it does, and so it should, if silence is all they hold. Man, even at his best, is not meant for absolute silence. For relative silence, for that stillness and serenity in which alone we can learn to face and love the truth about ourselves and about all created things, yes. For absolute silence, no. Absolute silence, in a human context, means one thing and one thing only: death. John Donne was right when he said that in 'the house and gate of heaven' there is 'no noise nor silence, but one equal music.' Total silence for us would be madness and annihilation. There must be a voice that answers; and our Christian faith is that even out of the silence of inter-stellar space comes such a voice.

And that in one way is what Christmas is all about. Ignatius, the martyr bishop who lived only seventy years after Christ himself, already understood this. Writing to the Christians at Ephesus he said: 'Hidden from the Prince of this world were the virginity of Mary and her child-bearing ... mysteries to be cried aloud, which were wrought in the silence of God.' Anything which God does is of necessity 'wrought in silence'. We cannot see where or how his finger touches the pulses of life; all we see is the new, miraculously transformed situation. Who in that crowd of 5,000 saw how or whence came the loaves and fishes? Who saw Jesus raised to life? No one. All men knew was that they had been hungry and were now satisfied; he had been dead and was now alive. And so it was at Christmas: 'How silently, how silently, the wondrous gift is given! So God imparts to human hearts the blessings of his heaven.' Or, in some very lovely words from the Apocrypha, which Christians early seized upon for use in their Christmas services: 'When all things were in quiet silence, and night was in the midst of her swift course, thine all-powerful Word leapt down from heaven, out of the royal throne.' This is the joy of Christmas: because Jesus was the Word out of silence who became flesh, no silence, neither of the grave nor of the infinite universe, can ever terrify us again.